MESOLITHIC LIVES IN SCOTLAND

MESOLITHIC LIVES IN SCOTLAND

GRAEME WARREN

TEMPUS

First published 2005

Tempus Publishing Limited
The Mill, Brimscombe Port,
Stroud, Gloucestershire, GL5 2QG
www.tempus-publishing.com

© Graeme Warren, 2005

The right of Graeme Warren to be identified as the Author
of this work has been asserted in accordance with the
Copyrights, Designs and Patents Act 1988.

All rights reserved. No part of this book may be reprinted
or reproduced or utilised in any form or by any electronic,
mechanical or other means, now known or hereafter invented,
including photocopying and recording, or in any information
storage or retrieval system, without the permission in writing
from the Publishers.

British Library Cataloguing in Publication Data.
A catalogue record for this book is available from the British Library.

ISBN 0 7524 3448 9

Typesetting and origination by Tempus Publishing Limited
Printed in Great Britain

CONTENTS

ACKNOWLEDGEMENTS

This book would not have been possible without the support of innumerable friends and family. In particular I would like to thank those who read drafts of the text: Chantal Conneller, Gabriel Cooney, Amber Godwin, Derek Hill and Caroline Wickham-Jones. This perceptive and varied set of readers would benefit any author. Their comments have transformed a rather creaky draft into, hopefully, a somewhat less creaky final text. I hope that they feel that I have done justice to their constructive critiques: of course, faults remaining are my responsibility alone.

I would like to thank colleagues in the School of Archaeology, University College Dublin, for providing such a supportive atmosphere in which to work. Bill Finlayson and Ian Ralston supervised my PhD, aspects of which are incorporated into this volume. Although we may have disagreed on details as well as general approaches, their critical support and encouragement of high standards has been empowering. Many other colleagues have helped to structure and refine my thoughts on the mesolithic in Scotland and archaeological practice beyond these confines: as well as the readers mentioned above, Mike Church, Mark Edmonds, Nyree Finlay, Melanie Giles, Aidan O'Sullivan, John Roberts, Rob Sands and Richard Tipping deserve special thanks. Peter Kemmis Betty also deserves thanks for his patience in tolerating the exceptionally late arrival of this book. I suspect it is of little consolation to him that I have missed more deadlines in writing this than in any other exercise I have ever undertaken.

My encounters with much of the material from eastern Scotland relied on collaboration with a variety of archaeological institutions and some collectors of artefacts. In particular it is appropriate to acknowledge the support of Neil Curtis, Marischal Museum, Aberdeen, for allowing me to work on the material from Forvie, and Neil and Liz for countless episodes of hospitality in Aberdeen and many discussions of aspects of archaeological practice. Alan Saville has facilitated many requests for access to material in the National Museum of Scotland; I enjoyed our discussions over lunchtime sandwiches. Bob Knox, now of the Peebles Archaeological Society, is enthusiasm personified and his willingness to share his carefully gathered collections of material is salutary.

Individuals and institutions have also been generous with either kind permission to use images or provision of images. I would like to thank and acknowledge: Alan Braby for figures 5, 11, 45, 50, 54 and 57; Walter Elliott for colour plate 16; Bill Finlayson for figure 39; Thomas Kador for colour plate 19; Meli Pannett for figure 52; the Peebles Archaeological Society for figure 56 and colour plate 10; Alan Saville for figure 23; Scotland's First Settlers for figure 6 and plates 6 and 18; Caroline Wickham-Jones for figures 54, 55 and 62 and plates 2, 20 and 21. I am grateful to the Society of Antiquaries of Scotland for permission to reproduce figures 2, 3, 23, 36, 41, 42 and 48.

Writing this book would not have been possible without the support of immediate family. Amber Godwin has had to deal with my curious interest in small stones and the lives of the long-dead for as long as she has known me. Her understanding, support and love mean more than I can say. Our baby girl, Sadhbh, deserves thanks too, not least for smiles, streams of random sounds and unconditional love.

The dedication of this book is a fulfilment of a long-awaited promise. In the early spring of 1995 I was sitting in a café in Kathmandu when, in a brief telephone call home, my mum told me that I had been offered a place on an MA course in Landscape Archaeology at the University of Sheffield: did I want to accept? I had recently graduated from Warwick and, distracted by many other interests (especially a very fine semi-acoustic bass guitar with flat wound strings), and with little real focus or direction, I had not done myself justice. My decision to return for postgraduate work was therefore somewhat surprising. On my return from travelling, and having already paid a deposit on a flat in Sheffield, I duly collected all the paperwork required for the Career Development Loan I intended to take in order to pay my fees. It was only on the night before I was to submit the paperwork that my parents asked to talk to me about money. We ran through my all-too-tight budget, and examined the details of the loan. In the end, we agreed that I would apply for a much, much smaller loan than originally planned. I still think that, in part, my parents acted more in hope than expectation and I remember asking them how I could thank them for this support; my dad's reply was simple – 'you can dedicate your first book to us'. As an inadequate token of thanks for support in so many ways, not just the financial, and in repayment of that promise, it is a real pleasure to dedicate this book to my parents, Linda and Barry Warren. I hope they enjoy it.

INTRODUCTION:
THE MESOLITHIC IN THE
MODERN WORLD

Perhaps you live in Aberdeen, in which case you may have walked along Broad Street and Queen Street, St Paul Street or The Green. Or maybe you know Peebles and have taken the popular footpath west, along the Tweed to the junction with the Manor Water at Manor Bridge. Perhaps you have fished some of the great salmon pools of the Tweed: at the Junction Pool, the productive Bemersyde and Ravenswood beats, or at the junction of the Tweed and the Ettrick. You may have visited Staffin Bay, on Skye; or walked at Cramond to the west of Edinburgh, visiting the Roman fort here or examining the fossil trees on the foreshore to the west, or moved further along the Forth, to Blackness Bay at Carriden. Possibly you have visited the neolithic funerary monuments at Camster in Caithness. In Dumfries and Galloway, you may have spent time at Luce Sands or Wig Sands; or perhaps you have preferred to visit Culbin Sands on the Moray coast. In Inverness you may have walked along Castle Street. Perhaps you know Oban and the high cliffs rising immediately behind the town. Possibly you have played golf on the links at Fife Ness, Fife; or maybe you have visited the island of Rùm, in the Inner Hebrides, or spent time on Jura, Islay, Oronsay, Arran or Risga. You may be a fan of malts from these islands. Maybe you have climbed Ben Lawers for the views across the Highlands. Perhaps you know the River Dee near Banchorry or have walked the Dee past Braemar. Maybe you have birdwatched at the Sands of Forvie in Aberdeenshire or fished for trout in the mouth of the Ythan here.

This seemingly random list of places, drawn from across the Scottish landscape, is linked by one simple fact. All of them are known to contain remains of the mesolithic period in Scotland and the list is far from exhaustive (1). The mesolithic, or middle stone age, is the first period of time during which archaeologists believe humans occupied the lands now called Scotland – some time between about 10,000 BC and 4000 BC. At this time Scotland was mainly covered in woodlands, and its occupants lived by gathering wild foods – they were hunter-gatherers not farmers. Most likely they were very mobile communities, who did not all live in one place for the whole year but moved with the seasons: sometimes in large groups, sometimes in smaller communities and families. Different resources were available in differing places at particular times of the year: some allowed large gatherings to take place, with attendant exchanges, marriages and conflicts. Other areas held only enough food for a family for a short while. Movement was by foot across the land, following paths through the varied woodlands that filled the plains,

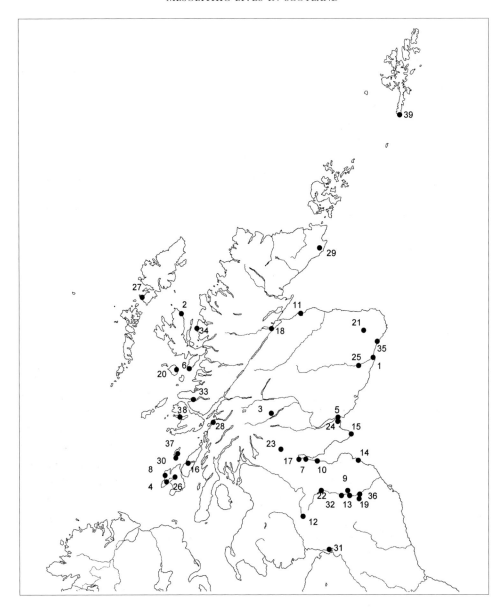

1 Locations of some of key mesolithic sites in Scotland. 1: Aberdeen (The Green, St Paul Street, Queen Street/Broad Street); 2: An Corran; 3: Ben Lawers; 4: Bolsay Farm, Gleann Mor; 5: Broughty Ferry; 6: Camas Daraich; 7: Carriden; 8: Coulererach; 9: Craigsford Mains; 10: Cramond; 11: Culbin Sands; 12: Daer; 13: Dryburgh Mains; 14: East Barns; 15: Fife Ness; 16: Glenbatrick; 17: Inveravon, Nether Kinneil; 18: Inverness (Muirtown, Castle Street); 19: Kalemouth; 20: Kinloch; 21: Little Gight; 22: Manor Bridge, The Dookits; 23: Meiklewood; 24: Morton; 25: Nethermills Farm; 26: Newton; 27: Northton; 28: Oban (Carding Mill Bay, MacArthur's Cave, Druimvargie); 29: Oliclett; 30: Oronsay (Caisteal nan Gillean, Cnoc Coig); 31: Redkirk Point; 32: Rink Farm; 33: Risga; 34: Sand; 35: Sands of Forvie; 36: Springwood Park; 37: Staosnaig; 38: Ulva Cave; 39: West Voe valleys and glens and by sea along rivers and from island to island. Many possessions travelled with people as they moved from place to place.

Archaeologists have long debated the extent of mesolithic settlement in Scotland. For many years, settlement appeared to be restricted to the coasts and some of the main river valleys, with little evidence of any settlement of the Northern and Western Isles. The difficulties of finding sites in the extreme north and west of Scotland are severe: peat formation and loss of coastlines since the mesolithic have masked or removed much of the mesolithic landscape. Yet mesolithic presence on Orkney is now well attested. Further north still, mesolithic activity on Shetland may be evidenced by oyster midden deposits at West Voe, Shetland (middens are accumulations of 'rubbish'), which date to the latest mesolithic or very earliest neolithic. Turning to the Western Isles, on Harris, evidence from Northton seems to indicate settlement in the mesolithic and Kevin Edwards and colleagues have long argued that the impact of hunting and gathering communities on the natural tree cover can be identified. Back on the mainland, recent discoveries of mesolithic material at Ben Lawers and high on the Dee above Braemar, as well as in the upper reaches of the Tweed and its tributaries, suggests routines of movement that covered much of the mainland as well.

Put simply, these recent discoveries confirm that mesolithic sites are found throughout Scotland, and the large number, and diverse location, of these sites across Scotland suggests that the landscape of these hunting and gathering communities lies very close to us as we go about our daily lives today. And yet, the mesolithic landscape is one that many people are very unfamiliar with: the ways in which mesolithic people understood the world, the stories they told about it and about each other, are lost from our memory. This book attempts to redress some of this loss. In it I focus very closely on the lives of those communities in the landscapes of Scotland, and attempt to resurrect some aspects of these people's lives. In so doing, I am keen to offer alternatives to more familiar ways of thinking about the Scottish landscape. But I must start with some basics: what is the mesolithic? What kinds of evidence are there for this period? As the book progresses these in turn change into other questions – how to gain an understanding of the character of people's lives in the distant past?

WHAT IS THE MESOLITHIC?

As stated above, the mesolithic is an archaeological term meaning 'middle stone age' (meso = middle, lithic = stone). The origins of the term lie in the nineteenth century, when early archaeologists defined large periods of time and characterised them according to types of material culture, economy and stages of 'civilisation'. Although there are debates about how best to define it, the mesolithic can broadly be understood to describe the period of time between the end of the last Ice Age and the arrival of farming. The period of time after the last Ice Age is also known as the Postglacial or the Holocene – it is our current geological time period. In archaeological terms, the mesolithic falls between the palaeolithic and the neolithic: the old and new stone ages respectively.

The palaeolithic is an enormously long period, encompassing early hominids in Africa, the expansion of members of the family *Homo* from Africa, and eventually, the origins of modern *Homo sapiens*. Somewhat closer to home, the upper palaeolithic saw modern humans arrive in Europe during the last Ice Age, very roughly speaking about 40,000 years ago, where they encountered, and eventually replaced, a different human species – *Homo neanderthalensis*. Following on from this, the hunter-gatherers of the upper palaeolithic, who lived in a landscape characterised by tundra and wide grassy plains, are now famous for their marvellous cave paintings, best known in France and Spain, but with recent discoveries in Britain.

Generally speaking, the neolithic in Europe falls after the Ice Age (which ended *c.* 9600 BC) and is associated with some technological changes, including pottery and formal architecture – but most importantly of all, with the invention of agriculture in the Middle East. In Europe the dates of the arrival of agricultural techniques varies in different areas, as people and ideas spread from the east. It is important to stress that Europe was not abandoned after the Ice Age, and that the spread of agriculture involved the interaction between new ideas and people and groups of indigenous hunter-gatherers: the peoples of mesolithic Europe. Sometimes, hunter-gatherer groups decided not to adopt farming when it was available, and continued with traditional economic

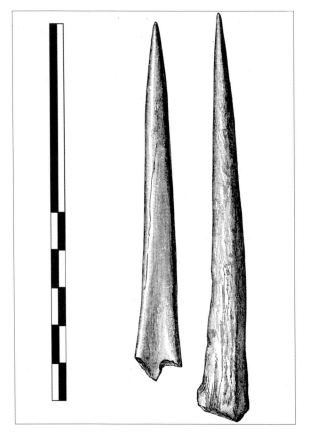

2 Bone points, Druimvargie.
Reproduced at 1:1. *After Anderson*

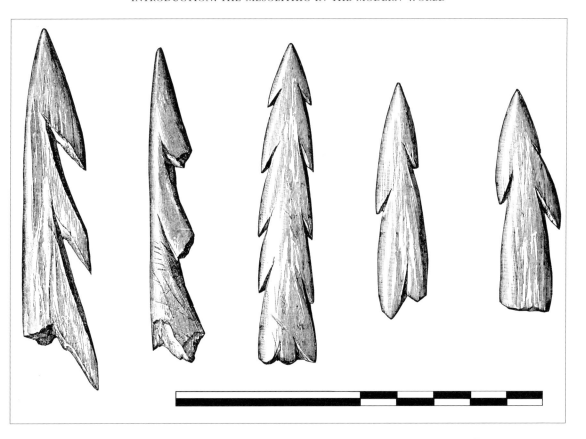

3 Fragmentary barbed points of antler from Druimvargie Cave, Oban, and Caisteal nan Gillean, Oronsay. The uniserial (barbs on one side) examples are from Druimvargie, and the biserial (barbs on both sides) from Caisteal nan Gillean. Reproduced at 1:1. *After Anderson 1898 Figs 1-2, 16-18*

routines for hundreds of years. Eventually people in most of temperate Europe did adopt farming: in Britain and Ireland this took place in the centuries around 4000 BC.

In north-west Europe, mesolithic communities therefore occupied postglacial environments for over 5000 years. They lived in a landscape mainly characterised by deciduous woodlands, and survived as hunters and gatherers, reliant on harvesting the resources of the world around them rather than growing their own plants and controlling domesticated animals.

WHAT KIND OF EVIDENCE IS THERE?

We'll be looking at the evidence from the mesolithic period throughout this book, but some general comments about the types of material present can be made first. Archaeologists estimate that about 90 per cent of material culture in hunter-gatherer societies was probably made of organic material – for example bone, animal skins or wood. However, Scotland

4 Worked stone from Manor Bridge, Scottish Borders. Scale bar at 1cm intervals. © *J. Rock*

has acidic soil and therefore organic material is generally destroyed with the passing of the years, unless it was deposited in exceptional circumstances (for some examples of organic materials, see *2* and *3*). The absence of organic materials is compounded by the fact that mesolithic communities in Scotland did not use pottery, a material which does survive well in the long term. The evidence for human lives in the mesolithic in Scotland is therefore often solely characterised by stone tools of different types (sometimes called 'lithics'), simply because these are more likely to survive (*4* and *colour plate 1*). Other materials do survive: some bone, antler and shell for example, but the dominance of stone tools as opposed to other materials is a major bias in archaeological understanding of the period. The 'Stone Age' only appears to be dominated by stone because of the survival of material – not because stone was the only thing that people used.

A further difficulty in finding remains from the period is that mesolithic people were fairly mobile – and some, at least, of their buildings were designed with this in mind (see chapter 6, and *5*). Mesolithic buildings were often (although not always) light constructions: there are no surviving upstanding mesolithic buildings and all that remains are a few holes where posts once stood ('post-holes'), a fireplace (or 'hearth') and some pits that once held varied deposits (*colour plate 2*). It is also important to note that this ephemeral evidence is very easily destroyed.

Hunter-gatherer sites are sometimes comprised of piles of empty shells from shellfish – often limpets, mussels and oysters. These accumulations, known as shell middens,

5 Reconstruction of a mesolithic activity area in the Scottish Borders. © *A. Braby*

6 Shell midden at Sand. © *Scotland's First Settlers*

create preserving alkali environments for bone and vary greatly in size and shape (6). Sometimes they includes worked bone – harpoons, bevel-ended tools or points. Most of the bones, however, are the remains of meals; burnt fragments of fish, mammals or birds. The careful analysis of these materials allows archaeologists to identify which species were killed and sometimes at what time of year. It is also important to note that the ways in which middens accumulate over time is informative about particular decisions being taken in the past. Shell middens, therefore, contain masses of information about hunter-gatherers, and are vital to making sense of mesolithic lives: much more than simple rubbish dumps, middens are a vital aspect of mesolithic archaeology. As hinted above, archaeologists also use environmental data to study the mesolithic, examining the histories of plants in a region, to see if the influence of hunter-gatherers can be spotted through disturbances to the natural sequence of vegetation.

A key point is that, in contrast to later periods of prehistory, the evidence from the mesolithic period is often described as fairly meagre, or even impoverished. From the neolithic of Scotland, for example, there are preserved buildings that one can walk into, funerary structures where the bones of the dead are laid out, pottery with elaborate decoration, or carvings made on stone. In contrast, it is clear that in the mesolithic we are often reliant on much less material. But to call the evidence impoverished is unfair, because if there's one thing we can say about the evidence from the mesolithic it is that there is sometimes an awful lot of it. At Staosnaig on Colonsay, for example, a recent excavation of a mesolithic site recovered 68,423 fragments of stone tools and manufacturing debris as well as 30-60,000 fragments of burnt hazelnut shells – hardly impoverished. Many other sites have even more lithics. The primary difficulty with the evidence from the mesolithic period in Scotland is not the material itself, but the widespread perception amongst archaeologists that it is intimately associated with fairly mundane economic activity: being basically tools for gathering food. There are a few items of personal adornment – some perforated cowrie shells from sites on the west coast, for example, that may have formed necklaces or other decoration – but a superficial review of the evidence offers very little in terms of explicit ritual or symbolic action that suggests how mesolithic people understood their world. In this, Scotland is very different from Scandinavia or France, which have examples of elaborate mesolithic burials, allowing an examination of symbolic understandings of death, as well as the analytical use of the skeleton as a source of information about diet and disease. There is no surviving mesolithic art in Scotland, not least because art would most likely have been on organic items – carved wood or dyed clothes. Thus it seems that discussions of the mesolithic of Scotland can only engage with the mundane remnants of economic activity rather than talk about ritual or symbolism: or about how people understood the world. This, in turn, is very revealing of modern attitudes to the world, namely the idea that we can separate economic activities from broader patterns of belief and spirituality. Yet in the past and in the present, people's identities, and the ways in which they understand the world, and each other, are formed and maintained through day-to-day habitual activity – getting on in the world. Rather than a weakness, the seemingly mundane character of the evidence is actually its strength – if approached in the appropriate fashion. One of the central issues this book explores is how a close-grained focus on the evidence allows the articulation of statements about people's lives in the distant past.

MAKING SENSE OF THE MESOLITHIC

It is important to note that interpretations of mesolithic material change over time, and that they often say as much about those doing the archaeology as they do about the past. For example, in the first half of the twentieth century archaeologists often interpreted the mesolithic (and other periods) through the use of what now seem very crude comparisons with hunter-gatherers in the contemporary world: these comparisons, known formally as ethnographic analogies, are a vital part of archaeological practice. In recent years the ways in which comparisons can be made between contemporary or near-contemporary communities of hunter-gatherers or farmers and the lives of the long-dead studied in archaeology has seen a great deal of critical attention. Early in the last century, however, this was not the case. Hunter-gatherers in particular were often perceived as 'savages', at the lowest rung of the ladder of civilisation. Ethnographic analogies, for example with supposedly similar hunter-gatherers in Tierra del Fuego, South America, were used to create an image of hunter-gatherers as 'strandloopers' – impoverished savages clinging to the edges of a heavily wooded country, subsisting on a miserable diet of shellfish and chance stranding of whales. Stuart Piggott, a great archaeological writer, and with a real talent for writing for a popular audience, presented a stark image of a heavily bearded mesolithic individual scavenging from a whale on a beach. It is an evocative and emotive icon.

Early accounts of the mesolithic argued that civilisation began with the arrival of the farming communities of the neolithic, who rapidly displaced the hunter-gatherers, cleared the forest, constructed stable villages and erected stone tombs. It is only too easy to see the attitudes of the Empire here: the equation of hunting and gathering ways of life with poverty, whilst change and development are associated with the arrival of outsiders. In the mid-twentieth century an important focus of archaeological analysis was identifying the 'cultural' background of mesolithic communities. Scholars such as Armand Lacaille, in his 1954 *The Stone Age in Scotland*, wrote of sites in the Tweed Valley as being 'derived ultimately from the Early and Middle Tardenoisian of the Continent', and of 'strains of Baltic Forest Culture'. In these kinds of interpretations, archaeologists attempted to identify large-scale similarities in material culture, and link distant communities as part of 'cultures', with stresses on migrations and movements of people. Thus 'Tardenoisian' refers to 'cultures' who manufactured certain kinds of stone tools first identified in France and 'Baltic Forest Culture' makes comparisons to the mesolithic of southern Scandinavia. Lacaille's stress on access routes across the landscape and immigration from different regions is also heavily influenced by the dominant military frameworks of the mid-twentieth century. Lacaille's classic work is very much a product of its time. In this, of course, Lacaille is no different to modern archaeologists. We are all a product of our particular historical circumstances, and the emphases of the stories we tell about the past always reflect the contexts within which we live. Future archaeologists may look back on this book and identify biases or themes that show how I am a product of the late twentieth and early twenty-first century. For example, my desire to show the wealth and potential of hunting and gathering communities in the past is undoubtedly a product of a post-colonial reappraisal of the nature of indigenous communities in the present. My stress on identity and meaning may be dismissed as a typically post-modern concern with identity politics, and a retreat from broader questions about evolution and historical process.

In the last 50 or so years the main focus of interpretations of the mesolithic has been on the character of the economy and on ecological questions, such as how hunter-gatherers adapted over time to changing environments. Partly because of the nature of the evidence, but also because of powerful preconceptions about the appropriate ways in which to study hunter-gatherers, the study of the mesolithic in Britain became obsessed with identifying the 'function' of sites in parts of wider systems of settlement – as a base camp, a hunting station or a stone working site. Working on the assumption that most hunter-gatherers are mobile people who move their settlements in order to procure different resources, British archaeologists built complex models in order to understand how mesolithic communities might have used their environment. Formidably intensive analyses of bone remains from sites were undertaken in order to identify which time of the year hunter-gatherers were present, and lengthy equations calculated the number of likely prey animals that might have been supported by a given type of woodland, and therefore the number of people that could live in this area. Many of these approaches are avowedly 'ecological' in their outlook, seeing many of the characteristics of hunter-gatherer society as determined by features of the environment. Most of these arguments are also very generalising, relying on common patterns of hunter-gatherer behaviour: sometimes it seems as if, because the evidence is 'meagre', the stress is placed on the system that supposedly links a particular archaeological site to wider patterns. As a consequence, the details of activity in a particular place are lost.

One of the beliefs that underpins this book and my archaeological practice is that the generalising functional approach to the mesolithic has not always helped in understanding people's lives in the past. Notwithstanding the advances that these approaches have brought us, all too often such accounts end up with an abstracted mesolithic population rather than any sense of how people grew up and learnt to act in the world. The aim of this book is to examine the ways in which mesolithic people came to understand their world and each other: this is an examination of mesolithic lives in Scotland. In it I hope to sketch a sense of the different ways in which people have lived in the seemingly familiar spaces with which this chapter opened – the landscapes of Scotland. It is this encounter that I see as the central joy of archaeology and it is caught well in a passage by the anthropologist Mary Steedley:

There is a kind of natural magic in landscape. The concrete traces of human experience enliven any terrain marked by human passage, however transient that passage may have been. Place names, paths, signs of habitation; the sense of space as formerly known or occupied (even if the presumed occupier is, today, unknown), an awareness, perhaps illusory, of the pulses of life and events that once animated an otherwise vacant terrain ... What I mean by natural magic: the sense that there is always another story embedded – slightly askew – just beneath the surface of the story that is being told.

Steedly, M. 1993. *Hanging Without a Rope: narrative experience in Colonial and Post Colonial Karoland*, p.147 (Princeton: Princeton University Press)

ALTERNATIVE MESOLITHIC LIVES

I therefore want to construct some alternative narratives of mesolithic lives in Scotland to give the general reader, or undergraduate student, a sense of the other stories embedded in the landscape. Rather than focus on generalising statements about kinds of mobility, or particular types of economic practice or symbolic beliefs, I would like to shift analytical attention and examine questions about social relations, identity and the ways in which people understood space and time.

This book therefore has three main aims: first and foremost this is an introduction to the mesolithic period in Scotland for people who are not familiar with it; secondly, as outlined above, I want to examine the mesolithic in terms of human lives in the past. This second aim is perhaps slightly unusual in the context of mesolithic archaeology, which is often dominated by generalisation. Therefore my third aim is to demonstrate some ways in which these new kinds of narratives might be constructed.

It is also worth being clear about two other decisions that structure the content of the book. Firstly, my primary engagement with the mesolithic of Scotland is an unusual one, in that I have worked on material from the east of the country, not the west. For a variety of reasons, including expectations of better preservation, mesolithic research in Scotland has focused heavily on the west of the country; introductory books often reflect this bias: the distribution map in Bill Finlayson's *Wild Harvesters*, for example, only identifies sites in the west and a general location of the River Tweed. My discussions incorporate much material from the east, and this may be one reason for a different flavour to my accounts. Secondly, I have deliberately avoided any detailed discussion of the neolithic in the main body of the text, especially in terms of the mesolithic-neolithic transition: the adoption of agriculture. This is not for lack of interest – the transition is a key research question: to deal with it properly would require another book of this length. However, the mesolithic has suffered from being perceived as a stepping stone to the neolithic, a period that is of little intrinsic interest, and with the transition an almost inevitable historical development that facilitated further progress. My decision to avoid discussion of the transition is simply an attempt to avoid this.

The book has eight chapters. Chapter 1, *Time and the mesolithic*, examines when the mesolithic was and discusses the evidence for the first settlement of Scotland. I then outline the importance of change within the mesolithic period, and the implications of the coarse-grained chronological resolution of the archaeological perspective. Chapter 2,

The changing landscape, focuses on the dynamic character of the Scottish landscape in the millennia following the Ice Age. Mesolithic communities in Scotland had to deal with changing sea levels, weather patterns, the migration of flora and fauna as well as dramatic short-term events. Reviews of these processes examine the scales at which these changes took place, asking whether people may have noticed them.

These chapters, therefore, provide a broad background to the mesolithic: what it was, when it was, and a generalised environmental context. Following on from this, the focus shifts to consider mesolithic lives in a more fine-grained way. Chapter 3, *Living among the trees*, begins this process by examining the ways in which woodlands may have structured mesolithic experience. This includes a more detailed examination of the character of mesolithic woodland, and discussion of ways of conceptualising the relationships linking people and the wooded landscape. This provides a useful context in which to discuss a key concept – the use of ethnographic analogies. Chapter 4, *The stuff of life*, examines the ways in which the hunter-gatherers of the mesolithic in Scotland obtained the necessary materials for life, from foodstuffs through medicine, to the raw materials for the manufacture of items of material culture, and asks how the procurement of resources can act as a key into the qualities of mesolithic lives. These themes, for example the ways in which skills and materiality coalesce in particular rhythms of labour, are returned to throughout the following chapters. In Chapter 5, *Craft and skill*, the explicit focus is on how craft and skill may have been linked to hunter-gatherers' perception of the world and their place in it. Chapter 6 examines the importance of *Space and place* in understanding mesolithic lives. Here I examine the influence of locations and architecture of different kinds on people's lives, from fireplaces and buildings through to the use of clearings and sacred hills. Chapter 7 examines community in the mesolithic, considering *The ties that bind* people to other people: family, kinship and wider associations. I also consider the ways that people may have thought about the dead and other animals. The *Epilogue* returns to consider the importance of identifying the real conditions of mesolithic lives in Scotland.

It is worth being explicit about the audience of this book and the expectations I have of them. This book is written with people who may have no prior knowledge of archaeology in mind, although I hope those with a smattering of knowledge will find it of interest. The opening chapters are very general, introducing forms of evidence and questions of scale. Yet by the end of the book, the key themes will be gender, identity and perception of the landscape: the cutting edge of mesolithic archaeology. At the end of each chapter I have created short dialogues to expand on some key areas: in many instances answering questions suggested by proofreaders of this book.

This is a book about interpretations; about some of the way that I enjoy thinking about the mesolithic in Scotland, which I sincerely hope will challenge the reader to think anew about a range of topics. It also, I hope, provides the reader with the information and framework to critically assess these interpretations, and build their own alternatives. To this end, further reading is suggested at the end of each chapter. Some of these are detailed, specialist texts. I firmly believe that archaeology is not a difficult subject, and that it does not require a long initiation and training to be involved with it. Yes, to become a skilled excavator, or understand the language and attentions to bizarre details of stone tool analysis, or to reconstruct the environment from pollen preserved in a bog requires a sustained period of instruction, preferably within a recognised framework. But the most basic skill of archaeology – thinking about how to understand human lives from the material remains they have left behind – is simply an extension of the interpersonal skills we use every day of our lives. I have tried to render the latest academic debates in relatively straightforward terms. I hope that this gives a sense of the excitement of these ideas, and of the joy of trying to make sense of the lives of the long-dead in Scotland. The best recommendation anyone can give this book is to follow these references, and to ask yourselves whether or not they help you make sense of mesolithic lives in Scotland. I think they do. It is, of course, only fair to warn the reader that I know that some colleagues would disagree with this approach to the mesolithic.

FURTHER READING

There are two excellent popular introductions to the archaeology of mesolithic Scotland. Caroline Wickham-Jones' *Scotland's First Settlers* (1994) and Bill Finlayson's *Wild Harvesters* (1998) are both highly recommended complements to this book. Bill Finlayson and Kevin Edwards also have a more scholarly paper (1997) with references to follow up, and a recent volume edited by Alan Saville includes a lot more detail (2004): Saville has also provided a detailed bibliography of the Scottish mesolithic (1998). Steve Mithen has written some introductory reviews of the mesolithic in Europe (1999) and Britain (1994). His most recent book *After the Ice* (2003) is a global take on the mesolithic – a readable account with some evocative fictions. Chris Smith's textbook (1992) offers a review of the British and Irish material, but takes a very different perspective to the one I give.

Finlayson, B. 1998. *Wild Harvesters: the first people in Scotland.* (Edinburgh: Canongate)

Finlayson, B. and Edwards, K. 1997. 'The Mesolithic' in K. Edwards and I.B.M. Ralston (eds) *Scotland: environment and Archaeology 8000BC-AD1000*, pp.109-125. (Edinburgh: John Wiley & Sons)

Mithen, S.J. 1994. 'The Mesolithic Age' in B. Cunliffe (ed.) *Prehistoric Europe: an illustrated history*, pp.79-135. (Oxford: Oxford University Press)

Mithen, S.J. 1999. 'Hunter-gatherers of the Mesolithic' in J. Hunter and I.B.M Ralston (eds) *The Archaeology of Britain: an introduction from the Upper Palaeolithic to the Industrial Revolution*, pp.35-57. (London: Routledge)

Mithen, S.J. 2003. *After The Ice: A Global Human History.* (Weidenfield & Nicholson)

Saville, A. (ed.) 2004. *Mesolithic Scotland and its Neighbours: the Early Holocene Prehistory of Scotland, its British and Irish context and some Northern European Perspectives.* (Edinburgh: Society of Antiquaries of Scotland)

Saville, A. 1998. 'Studying the Mesolithic Period in Scotland: a Bibliographic Gazetteer' in N. Ashton, F. Healey and P. Petit (eds) *Stone Age Archaeology: Essays in Honour of John Wymer*, pp.211-224. (Oxford: Oxbow Monograph 102/Lithic Studies Society Occasional Paper 6)

Smith, C. 1992. *Late Stone Age Hunters of the British Isles*. (London: Routledge)

Wickham-Jones, C.R. 1994. *Scotland's First Settlers*. (London: Batsford/Historic Scotland)

AN INTERJECTION

OK. So this is all about the mesolithic in Scotland, and you're telling me that there are all kinds of wonderful things that we can find out about these hunter-gatherers and the way they made sense of the world. But I'm finding it hard to get a frame of reference: I don't really know what these people were like at all at this stage. What kind of communities did they live in? How many of them were there? Were they just like us? You mentioned 'savages' earlier and seemed upset that some archaeologists have used ideas like this — but surely people living this long ago were much less complex than we are?

Good questions, and hard to answer in brief. I hope that reading the book will help. I'm loath to paint a detailed picture at this stage, as I'd rather lead you through the material at different scales, allowing this kind of understanding to emerge through encounters with the evidence.

But you're right, some generalisations would probably help. The first key point is that the mesolithic was, in some ways, populated by people like us: *Homo sapiens*. Mesolithic people had all of the same biological possibilities as us, they spoke complex languages, with all of the potential for symbolism this entails, and they engaged in complex social relationships.

Questions about community size are difficult to deal with in the abstract: they changed over different timescales. This is examined in more detail in chapter 7. In general we are probably talking about people who lived at fairly low population levels, and who moved around the landscape in a lot in different ways and for different reasons. There is debate about how much internal differentiation there may have been in these communities: put simply, there is limited evidence for this at this stage in Britain, although the picture on the continent is slightly different.

More importantly, these were communities for whom day-to-day life depended on their acute perception of the world that surrounded them: the qualities of resources available, how to identify stone sources or areas of productive fishing. These skills resulted from experience: from the ways in which individuals grew within a particular context. Crucially, these skills and abilities were also suffused with a variety of other understandings: of the relationships between the spirits, of time depth and the appropriate ways of acting for particular kinds of people. It is these kind of relationships that are crucial to gaining an understanding of mesolithic people and, really, that's the focus of this book.

I

TIME AND THE MESOLITHIC

I begin by outlining when the mesolithic took place, both in Britain generally and in Scotland specifically. This chapter examines issues relating to the time and the study of the mesolithic in Scotland, and within this context examines the controversial evidence for the first settlement of Scotland. The focus then shifts to considering the importance of recognising change within the mesolithic period and the issue of time resolution in mesolithic archaeology, as well as the implications this has for understandings of people's lives in the past.

WHEN WAS THE MESOLITHIC?

We have established that the mesolithic is the period of time between the end of the last Ice Age and the start of farming. Although this seems simple, even such a straightforward statement covers many archaeological controversies. For example, and as discussed below, the question of when the mesolithic begins in an area is very difficult to assess, and in some senses, rather meaningless. The end of the mesolithic is also an area of considerable discussion, with debate on the timing and extent of transformation associated with the arrival of agricultural techniques in a region. This section outlines the Scottish and British evidence for when the mesolithic is, introducing key concepts in turn.

Firstly, however, it is important to note that dating of archaeological materials is not exact. In the days before scientific dating, elaborate schemes linking certain kinds of artefacts into 'cultures' were a key aspect of the establishment of chronologies. The origins of the term 'mesolithic' lie in these kind of archaeological developments: the mesolithic is a short-hand for a range of more-or-less similar artefact assemblages associated with postglacial environments. Although scientific dating is now much the preferred way of establishing the age of the site, archaeologists are still often reliant on looking at artefacts and working out roughly how old they might be. Archaeologists have frequently supposed that particular kinds of artefacts are characteristic of particular periods of time, and that the presence of these artefacts in a particular place means they were occupied at this time.

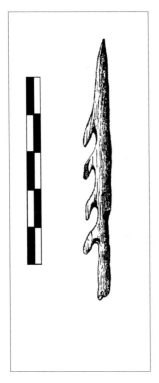

7 Uniserial barbed point, supposedly from 'Glenavon'. Reproduced at 1:1. *After Lacaille 1954 Fig 71*

Of course, caution is sometimes required. Figure 7 shows the 'Glenavon' barbed point. The Glenavon point is uniserial – it has barbs on only one side, and certain of its formal properties are broadly paralleled with European artefacts dating to the early mesolithic or late glacial. Thus its date is established by typological comparisons. 'Glenavon' has been understood to be in Banffshire (although there are other Glenavons in Scotland). However, the Glenavon point formed part of a collection gifted by Henderson-Bishop, a prolific collector of archaeological materials, to the Hunterian Museum in Glasgow. The point was discussed in letters exchanged between Henderson-Bishop and the curator, Anne Robertson. Henderson-Bishop concludes that 'the "Glenavon" harpoon always seemed to me doubtful, I do not remember how I got it. If I labelled it, it was on the authority of the seller, but it was probably labelled when I got it.' Henderson-Bishop purchased items from all across Scotland and Europe, and lived in Switzerland where he worked on palaeolithic material. The Glenavon bone point is dubious evidence for early activity and serves as a useful reminder that archaeological objects can have complex histories in the recent past, as well as the distant past.

Even at their best, typological dates, reliant on comparing material across large areas, are often very broad and vague, but because many artefacts are found without any material that can be used for a scientific date, the use of artefact-based dates is still very important: many of the detailed names for particular kinds of artefacts are very helpful in establishing these kinds of comparisons. The jargon of archaeological analysis, although intimidating, can therefore be helpful. The earliest evidence for settlement in Scotland includes further examples of this kind of argument.

Since the 1950s archaeologists have used various scientific dating techniques in order to find out the age of sites and artefacts. By far the most important of these techniques for the mesolithic is radiocarbon dating, which allows a good estimate of the true age of a site. Again, there are difficulties here. The radiocarbon age of a site is not the same as its calendar age (see discussion at the end of this chapter for details), and some books are rather unclear on which kind of dates they are using. In this book, all dates are in calendar years, i.e. a date of 8300 BC means something that took place 10,305 years ago (as I write this in 2005). An important illustration of this problem comes with a key date: the end of the last Ice Age and the sudden onset of warm conditions at the start of the Holocene (the present geological time period). Most writers agree that this change took place at 10,000 radiocarbon years ago. But this is a radiocarbon age, which, if you convert it to calendar years, works out somewhere around 9600 BC, give or take a few centuries: in other words about 11,600 years ago.

Regardless of these problems, there are difficulties with trying to place neat dates on the mesolithic. The last chapter suggested that the mesolithic could be defined as postglacial hunter-gatherers. Therefore, one might expect that the mesolithic begins at around 9600 BC. But is it possible to use this broad age as the start of the mesolithic? In lowland England, for example, it is clear that hunters and gatherers were present in late glacial times, about 13000 BC, exploiting wide, grassy and tundra-like plains (the evidence in Scotland is more controversial, as we will see below). These people would probably be classified as 'palaeolithic'. And yet it is clear that their descendants adapted to the changing landscapes as the Ice Age ended, eventually becoming adept hunter-gatherers of woodlands. Clearly, it would be futile to try and draw a hard and fast line between palaeolithic and mesolithic in this kind of context, or to say that after a certain date people became mesolithic. Did somebody who was palaeolithic have a mesolithic child? Of course not: these are varied communities of hunter-gatherers who were living in different environments at different times, and the archaeological labels are simply very crude. Luckily, in Scotland the issue of continuity from palaeolithic to mesolithic is made a little simpler by the scarcity of evidence for pre-Holocene, or palaeolithic, occupation.

The end of the mesolithic is also ambiguous and controversial. Traditionally archaeologists had seen the onset of the neolithic in an area as witnessing the end of hunter-gatherers and the arrival of the first farmers. The neolithic was seen to bring technical advances – pottery, monumental architecture and domesticated plants and animals – and was often associated by archaeologists with colonising movements of farming communities. More recently archaeologists have argued that hunter-gatherers *chose* to take up farming, or have examined how farmers and hunter-gatherers might have lived together for periods of time. Other archaeologists have questioned the importance of the change in the economy, stressing instead the arrival of new items of material culture and belief systems in transforming hunting and gathering communities. It is easy to see how discussions of this type have complicated any attempt to identify the 'end' of the mesolithic. Nevertheless, in a British context, a date of around 4000 BC is a reasonable marker. Some changes may have begun before this date, and a very rapid transition to farming takes place a few centuries after it, but as shorthand, 4000 BC is useful.

It is important to be clear about what our terms are. The word mesolithic is merely a modern label for a period of time. No one in the past thought of themselves as mesolithic, and it is a rather crude label for a diverse group of hunting and gathering communities. Furthermore, attempts to place rigid dates on these groups are fraught with difficulty. In any case, I suspect that we should probably worry less about labels, and think more about the character of people's lives in prehistoric Scotland. The evidence from Scotland is detailed in just a moment, looking more closely at the dates of the first settlers and when farming might have arrived, but first it is important to place this in a broader British and Irish context: Scotland's first settlers must have come from somewhere.

THE LATEST UPPER PALAEOLITHIC AND THE MESOLITHIC IN THE BRITISH ISLES

The end of the last Ice Age was characterised by warmer and colder spells. Current models of the climate suggest that there was a warm spell towards the end of the last Ice Age; dating to somewhere between 13-11000 BC, and known as the late glacial interstadial period. A cold period, known as the Loch Lomond Stadial or Younger Dryas (c.11,000-9600 BC), followed and this, in turn, was followed by the rapid warming which is often taken to mark the end of the Ice Age (crudely speaking around 9600 BC), with plants and animals soon migrating into the new areas. (A stadial is a cold glacial period and interstadial a warm period. There is great debate about whether we are currently living after the Ice Age, or simply in a convenient interstadial.) During the late glacial and the very early postglacial the landscape of north-west Europe was very different from today. Not only was the area mainly characterised by light scrub, grassland or tundra vegetation but, on a global scale, vast quantities of water were caught up in ice caps and the sea level was dramatically lower than it is at present. In fact, sea level was so low that much of the North Sea was a low-lying dry plain, joining the British Isles to the rest of continental Europe.

The earliest evidence for the resettlement of the British Isles after the last Ice Age comes soon after the beginnings of the late glacial interstadial. A number of sites across England and Wales, but not from the upland areas of Britain, include characteristic 'Creswellian' stone tool assemblages named after a key site at Creswell Crags, Derbyshire. These assemblages include large flint blades, elongated, parallel-sided flakes of material carefully and skilfully struck from cores (8). There are also a suite of distinctive artefacts made by modifying or 'retouching' the edges of blades and flakes (9 and 10). The distribution of these sites, and the low sea levels at this time, seem to suggest people moving into Britain across the North Sea plain. Faunal assemblages of this period include mammoth and reindeer, as well as species such as artic hare, indicating a cold, open landscape. Recently (2003) the first British cave art was discovered in Creswell Crags – a depiction of a stag, and possible representations of birds. These are likely to date to this period, and indicate the close connections between the late-glacial settlers of Britain and the upper palaeolithic communities that lived in Europe. It seems likely that these people lived a very mobile lifestyle, and faunal evidence suggests that wild horse was a key resource with red deer also significant.

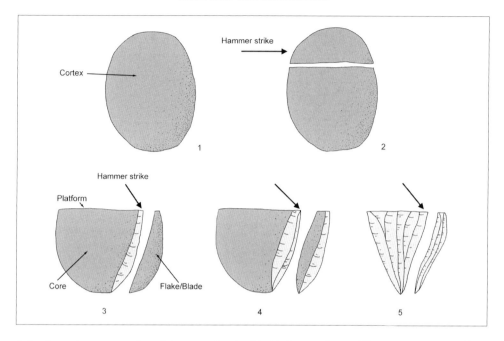

8 A schematic representation of the stages involved in blade manufacture. The sequence starts with a flint pebble with its characteristic battered outside, or cortex (1). The pebble is split open with a hard blow (2) the clean interior surface is then used as a 'platform' – the surface that the hammer strikes in order to remove further blades and flakes. This sequence begins in (3), with a hammer blow onto the platform removing an elongated flake – or blade. The outside of this flake/blade is completely covered with cortex. Further removals use ridges caused by the first removal, to help guide the force of the blow. Thus (4) shows a blow removing another blade, which has cortex on half of its exterior surface. This sequence continues, until all cortex is removed, ultimately leading to the formation of a classic pyramid shaped core (5). Analysis of the proportion of cortex in an assemblage helps archaeologists to understand the ways that stone-tool technology was organised across the landscape

In the centuries following 12000 BC birch and willow woodland became more significant parts of the landscape, and some open grassland species, such as the mammoth, appear to have become extinct. The changes in the environment must have led to some changes in the structures of people's lives. For example, although stone-tool industries are still based on the production of blades, a different, if still related, range of retouched pieces are now manufactured. The extent of settlement during the Younger Dryas cold period (*c.*11000–9600 BC) is unclear, although a range of characteristic finds, and some radiocarbon-dated bone indicates some activity in the south and east of England. Settlement may have become less intensive, although evidence of a large-scale 'gap' or break in traditions of settlement in the land now called Britain is not clear. Some writers, such as Nick Barton, argue that there is continuity in the kinds of stone tools manufactured in the 'late glacial' or 'final upper palaeolithic' and the 'mesolithic'. With rapid warming at the end of the Younger Dryas, mesolithic settlement of the British Isles appears rapidly.

The most famous early mesolithic site in the British Isles is Star Carr, in North Yorkshire. Here hunter-gatherers made extensive use of a large lake and its surrounds

9 Turning a blade into a scraper. Upper left and right show the two surfaces of a cortical blade (platform to top). In the lower left direct hard hammer percussion is being used to remove small flakes from the end of the blade, creating the curved working 'scraper' edge visible in the lower right. The small flakes and shatter result from this process

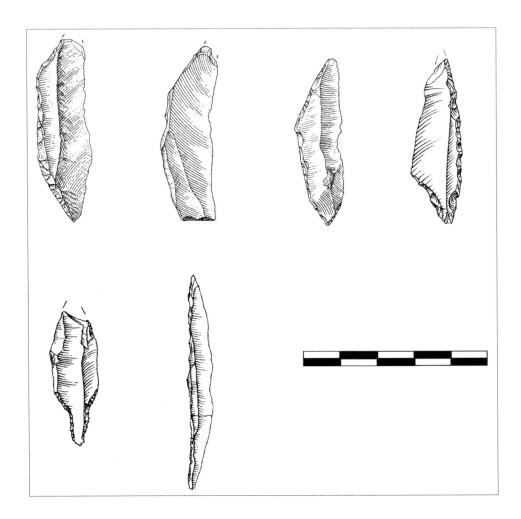

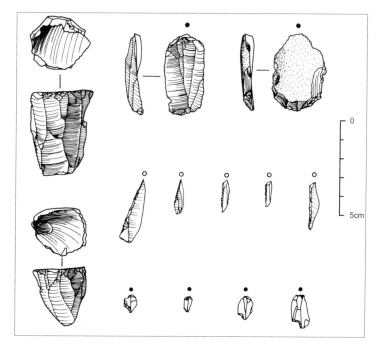

Opposite below: 10 Characteristic artefacts of the late glacial period in southern Britain. Upper row, left to right: Cheddar Point (Creswellian), curve backed point, angle backed point, penknife point (all final upper palaeolithic). Lower row, left to right: Ahrensburgian point, backed bi-point (final upper palaeolithic). Reproduced at 1:1. *Combined and rescaled image from Barton 1997 Figs 97, 101, 108*

Above: 11 Stone tools from the Sands of Forvie, Aberdeenshire. Upper row: left; blade core, centre and right; scrapers. Middle row: microliths. Lower row: left; blade core; microburins. Reproduced at 1:2. © *A. Braby*

around 8800-8500 BC. The site was located immediately on the lakeshore, with birch scrub in the area. Star Carr is especially important because it is a 'wet', or waterlogged, site. Wet archaeological sites preserve organic materials – for example wood, bone and antler – and give a much more rounded picture of hunter-gatherer life than is possible from stone remains alone. At Star Carr, for example, a walkway was constructed at the edge of the lake, possibly to improve access for boats. There is evidence of people deliberately burning lakeside vegetation to improve access or visibility. Recent reinterpretations of Star Carr by Chantal Conneller demonstrate that the site is important as a place for depositing certain kinds of animal remains – especially those relating to animals' heads – possibly indicating the importance of animals in the symbolic worlds of mesolithic communities of this time. But this was not just a ritual area: many other activities took place, including the working of antler into various kinds of tools and the hunting of aurochs (wild cattle), as well as red deer, roe deer, elk and wild pig.

The British mesolithic is traditionally divided into two periods: early and late. This division describes changes in the stone-tool technology of the two periods, especially

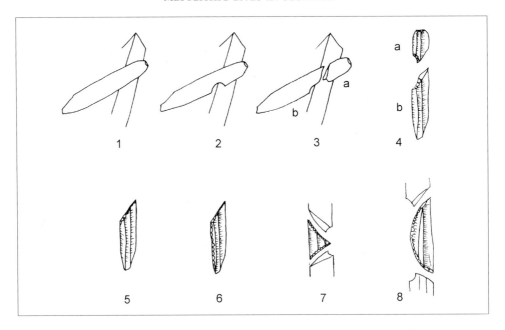

12 A schematic representation of microlith manufacture. In 1–3 a blade is weakened by creating a notch on one side, and snapping at this point of weakness. The two resulting pieces (4a, 4b) or 'microburins' are characteristic of microlith manufacture. This process allows standardisation of the size of microliths. Following from the snapping, the addition of small amounts of further steep edge retouch creates the distinctive shapes of different microlith types: (5) obliquely blunted, (6) scalene triangle. Combinations of notch and angle of snap and retouch create forms such as the isosceles triangle (7) and crescent (8). *After Inizan et al. 1992 Fig 33 with modifications*

in terms of microliths, which were but one of a range of different kinds of stone tools manufactured at the time (*11*). Microliths (literally 'small stone') are the most characteristic stone tool type of the mesolithic period in the British Isles. Stone-tool production is discussed in more detail in chapter 5, but microliths are carefully manufactured implements made into particular shapes (*12, 13* and *14*). Stone workers carefully produced blades. Some of these were used in this form, but others were snapped into smaller length pieces, and had some of their edges blunted. Archaeologists have been obsessed about the size and shape of microliths, and a plethora of different terms describe particular shapes. These terms – scalene triangle, obliquely truncated points, hollow based points, rods – can seem intimidating to the uninitiated: it is important to note that the need to pigeonhole microliths into certain types is a hangover from the days when formal artefact types and typologies were central to the construction of chronologies.

Microliths are tiny (*15*); anything from 4–5cm in size down to less than 1cm, and they were probably used as part of compound or composite tools. A knife, for example, might contain a row of five or six microliths. According to analyses of patterns of damage found on their edges, microliths seem to have been used for many different purposes, although many archaeologists have falsely supposed that their main use was in hunting. 'Early' mesolithic sites have 'broad blade' microliths, mainly fairly large examples and with some

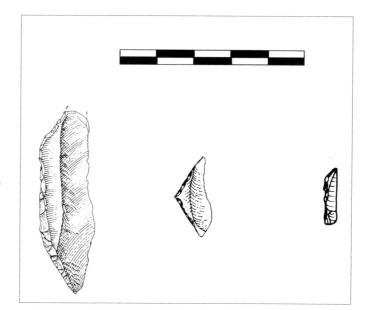

13 A crudely simplified depiction of changing forms of retouched blades from the Creswellian (a Cheddar Point, Barton 1998), into the early mesolithic (an isosceles triangle from Morton A, Coles 1971) and the late mesolithic (a scalene triangle from Forvie)

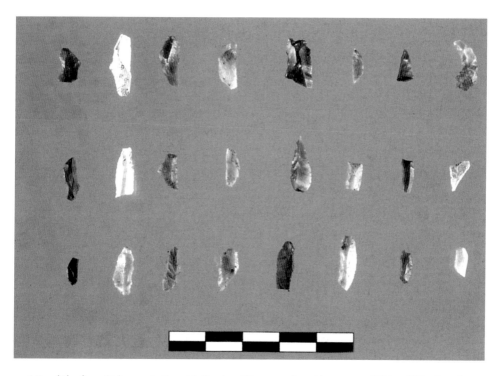

14 Microliths from Kalemouth, Scottish Borders. These artefacts form part of Walter Elliott's surface collection from the site, now lodged with the National Museum of Scotland. Scale bar at 1cm intervals. © *J. Rock*

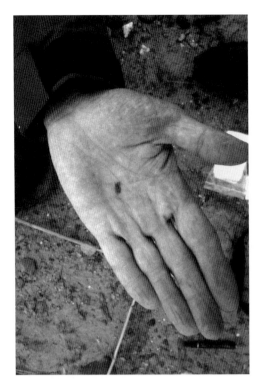

15 Fragment of scalene triangle microlith recovered by Graham Steele during fieldwork at the Sands of Forvie. The microlith fragment is approximately half its full size. © G. Warren

particular shapes important, especially large triangles (isosceles) and blades with blunting at an oblique angle (obliquely truncated/blunted points). 'Later' mesolithic industries are very diverse, but often have much smaller microliths made into geometric shapes: also known as 'narrow blade' (see *13*). The change, which probably took place around 8000-7500 BC, is often interpreted as indicating a shift in hunting strategy and technology due to the development of denser woodlands over time, although this explanation may be a little simplistic for the British Isles as a whole. It is important to recognise that 'early' and 'late' mesolithic are, yet again, crude labels: as discussed below, some Scottish sites do not appear to fit easily into these frameworks.

SCOTLAND'S FIRST SETTLERS?

The date by which people first arrived in Scotland is controversial and can only be understood in a wider archaeological and environmental context. The review of the British Isles above shows that through the late glacial warm and cold spells evidence for settlement seems to be limited to the lowland south and east: Ireland and Scotland, as well as much of upland Wales have little clear evidence of human settlement. In the absence of clear evidence some more ambiguous material has become the object of debate.

This includes distinctive stone tools found in Orkney, Islay, Jura, Tiree and most recently in Wester Ross. These small points have a distinctive 'tang' created by retouching their

1 Cores and débitage from the Sands of Forvie, Aberdeenshire. *Photograph taken by Rob Sands;* © *G. Warren*

2 Excavation of pit containing a cache of coarse stone tools and pebbles at Kinloch, Rùm. © *Caroline Wickham-Jones*

Above: 3 View to Manor Bridge, Scottish Borders, from south. The site at Manor Bridge lies on a rocky outcrop above the Tweed and the ridge behind this outcrop. The junction of the Tweed, which is flowing towards the viewer, and Manor water is immediately in front of Manor Bridge. © *G. Warren*

Right: 4 Modern birch woodland, Burn of Calleter, Angus. © *G. Warren*

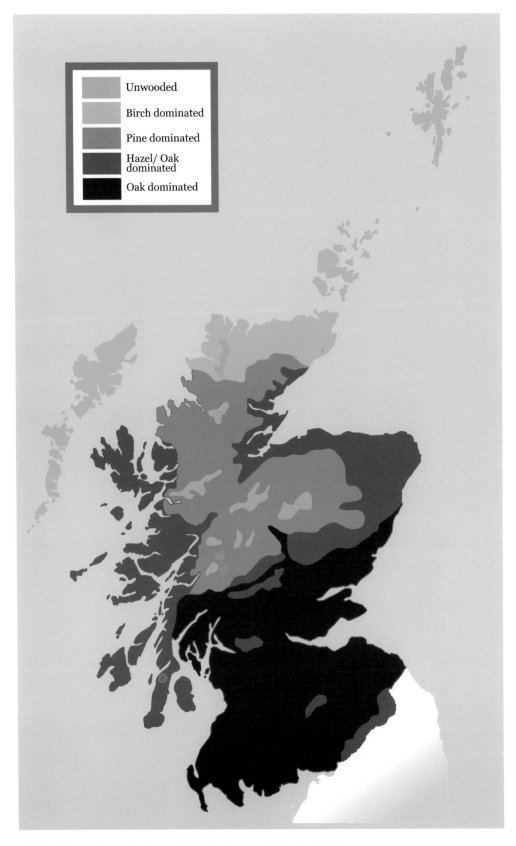

5 Distribution of woodland types in Scotland, *c.*4000 BC. *After Tipping 2004*

6 Rockshelter at Sand. © *Scotland's First Settlers*

7 St Mary's Loch, Scottish Borders. Mesolithic artefacts are known from near the loch and the Yarrow Valley leading to it. Note the alluvial fan formed by sediment carried down the Crosscleuch River, now occupied by the Tibbie Shiels Inn

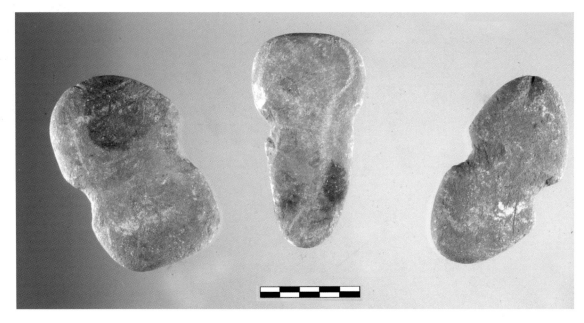

8 Waisted pebbles from Rink Farm, Scottish Borders. Scale bar at 1cm intervals. See discussion in text for problems in interpreting these artefacts. *From Walter Elliott's collection.* © *J. Rock*

9 Path in woodland. © *G. Warren*

10 Stone tools from Manor Bridge, Scottish Borders. The range of raw materials used at Manor Bridge (chert, flint, chalcedony and others) is characteristic of the Tweed Valley mesolithic. The range of raw materials is very useful analytically. © *Peeblesshire Archaeological Society*

Above: 11 The Dookits, near Pebbles, Scottish
Borders. Mesolithic artefacts are found on and
above this rock outcrop by the River Tweed.
© *G. Warren*

Right: 12 Bob Knox and members of the
Peebles Archaeological Scoiety examining
material at Clashpock Rig, Scottish Borders. This
fluvioglacial terrace contains chert and worked
material has been found at the site in an area of
known early prehistoric activity. © *G. Warren*

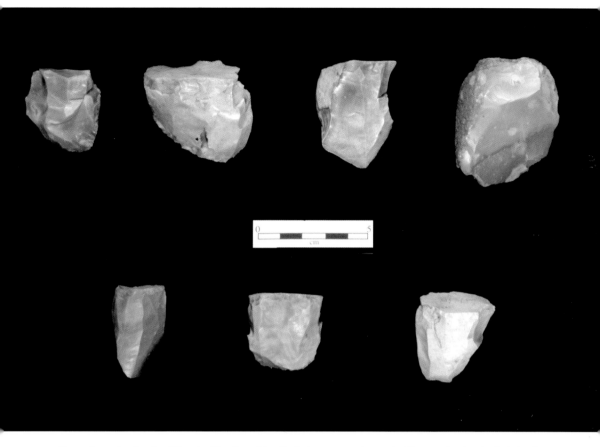

15 Cores from the Sands of Forvie, Aberdeenshire. Scale bar at 1cm intervals. *Photograph taken by Rob Sands,* © *G. Warren*

Opposite above: 13 Seascape, from Scourie. Negotiating the complex interplay between land and sea, characteristic of the Scottish coasts, likely formed an important part of people's skills and routines. © *G. Warren*

Opposite below: 14 View to Flint Hill, Scottish Borders. Exposures of chert on Flint Hill were quarried in early prehistory, possibly in the mesolithic. Scheduling the procurement of different resources, some found only in specific locations, formed the basic rhythms of mesolithic life. © *G. Warren*

16 Microliths from Rink Farm, Scottish Borders. © *W. Elliott*

17 View of lithic bearing surfaces at the Sands of Forvie, Aberdeenshire. © *G. Warren*

18 Excavation of shell midden deposits at Sand. © *Scotland's First Settlers*

Above: 19 View of western Scotland from Red Bay, Co. Antrim, Northern Ireland. © *T. Kador*

Left: 20 View of Bloodstone Hill. © *Caroline Wickham-Jones*

21 Lithics from Rùm, varied materials. *Wickham-Jones 1990: frontispiece,* © *C. Wickham-Jones*

22 Pitchstone from surface collections at varied sites along the Tweed Valley, Scottish Borders. Scale bar at 1cm intervals. © *J. Rock*

Above: 23 Seal at Loch Laxford.
© *G. Warren*

Right: 24 View of excavations at Sands of
Forvie, Aberdeenshire, 2001. © *G. Warren*

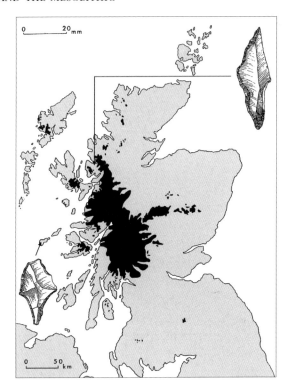

16 Find spots of reliable Ahrensburgian type points in relation to extent of Loch Lomond Stadial ice cover (black). Upper scale for artefacts; lower scale for base map. *After Ballin & Saville 2003*

base to form a blunt point, which was probably used for hafting purposes. Some writers think that these pieces are the same as late glacial points characteristic of reindeer hunting groups from continental Europe: these are 'Ahrensburgian' assemblages, named after a town near Hamburg. Broadly speaking, the Ahrensburgian dates to the later half of the Younger Dryas, and into the start of the Holocene. In Scotland this cold period was characterised by ice re-advancing in the Highlands and the Southern Uplands (16): conditions may have been as much as 20°c colder on average than at present. Away from the ice, most of Scotland must have been bare of vegetation, or broadly tundra-like: a seemingly harsh and unwelcoming environment; although the seasonal richness of Arctic environments today should be noted when imagining these early landscapes.

Some archaeologists have suggested that the location of the finds of tanged points along the western seaways of Scotland indicates the importance of marine resources to early settlers. Others argue that in a European context, Ahrensburgian settlements are frequently closely associated with evidence of reindeer hunting. In this context it is important to note that reindeer survived in Scotland until at least *c.*7000 BC. However, others are not convinced by the links to the Ahrensburgian, and argue that the similarities between the Scottish and European artefacts are coincidental, or that the parallels are not to late glacial Germany, but to early mesolithic stone industries in northern Scandinavia. These arguments show the difficulties of comparing isolated artefacts across large distances in the absence of a properly dated site. Recently Alan Saville and Torben Ballin have offered a detailed review suggesting that the artefacts from Tiree and Wester Ross are likely to be genuine (see *16* for locations). Overall however, at present the question of late glacial settlement must remain open. The possibility of occasional visits northwards from people living further south is strong, but even if people were in Scotland at this time, archaeologists can say little in detail about their lives.

Although it is assumed that the Loch Lomond Stadial saw little human settlement of Scotland there seems no strong reason that hunter-gatherers could not have occupied Scotland very rapidly at the end of the Ice Age (i.e. sometime immediately following 9600 BC). As detailed in the next chapter, the warming of the climate was rapid, and Scotland would have become a much more habitable and rich landscape as plant and animal communities migrated north and west. However, there is little clear evidence for early mesolithic activity in Scotland, and the first radiocarbon dated site is Cramond, on the shores of the Forth, dates to about 8500-8300 BC. This gap of about 1000 years is very striking and numerous attempts have been made to fill it.

As noted above, the mesolithic of Britain is conventionally split into 'early' and 'late' on the basis of stone tool typology. In Scotland, evidence for 'early' mesolithic activity is normally identified through such comparative analyses. In fact, one of the most interesting things about the early mesolithic are very large-scale similarities in material culture across the North Sea plain – the stone tool industries at Star Carr, North Yorkshire, and Duvensee, Germany, for example, are surprisingly similar. Most archaeologists have supposed that these similarities are evidence of very mobile groups of hunter-gatherers who kept in contact across very long distances.

In Scotland, some writers have argued that stone tools from the site of Morton, Fife, are very similar to those used at Star Carr and are therefore broadly of that date. Morton is a complex site, which was re-occupied much later on in the mesolithic, disturbing the earlier deposits. Based on sea level change in the region (see chapter 2), Clive Bonsall has argued that the early occupation of Morton took place before about 8500 BC: this date is in keeping with the character of the stone tools. Stone-tool industries from sites such as Glenbatrick I on Jura, or Craigsford Mains, in the Tweed Valley, may also show evidence of these early mesolithic traditions although it remains difficult to identify and isolate an 'early' mesolithic site. Despite these problems, the arguments for some kind of 'early' activity are more convincing than those claiming late glacial occupation, and seem to imply some kind of 'early mesolithic' presence in Scotland in the centuries following the end of the Loch Lomond Stadial, even if this cannot be dated very clearly. Furthermore, detailed understandings of how these people lived in Scotland are absent. In this sense, it is clear that the quest for the earliest site in Scotland is not really as important as a broader understanding of which direction people moved from, and why.

Bill Finlayson has pointed out that, whilst we have lots of evidence of later mesolithic occupation, we have little evidence of anything earlier. Finlayson argues that to understand the initial colonisation of Scotland we must consider people's motives. The landscapes of Europe at this time were very different (*17*, see chapter 2 for detail), with Scotland the mountainous end of a large area of rolling hills and plains – the European lowlands. The key focus of people's lives at the time appears to have been the large mammals of these lowlands – Scotland may have been relatively peripheral to people's

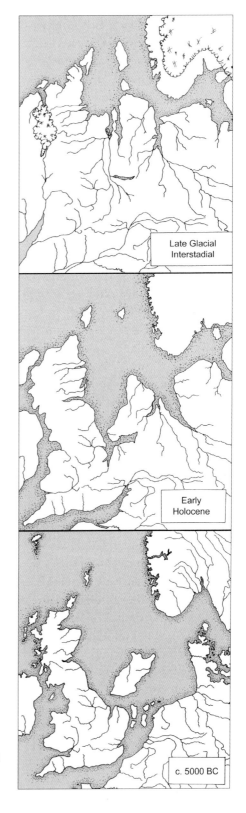

17 Reconstructions of changing sea, land and ice relationships on the North Sea plain, or 'Doggerland'. *Redrawn after Coles 1998*

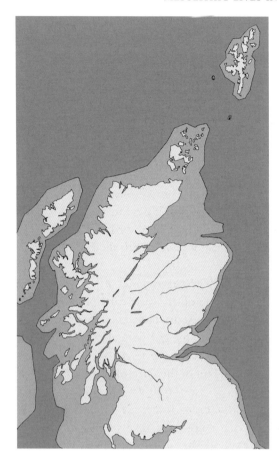

Left: 18 Land loss in Scotland since the beginning of the mesolithic. *Redrawn after Ashmore 2004*

Below: 19 Excavations at Daer Reservoir, Lanarkshire. Careful survey directed by Tam Ward of the shorelines exposed at times of low water level led to the discovery of one of the oldest sites in Scotland. © *G. Warren*

concerns at this time. If there was no population pressure on these groups there may have been little reason to fully settle Scotland at this time.

A possible parallel can be seen in the colonisation of north and western Norway. Here deglaciation left an exceptionally rich artic maritime environment available for exploitation by hunter-gatherers from the late glacial period. However, there was a delay until round about 9000 BC when people first began to settle in the area. Hein Bjerck has argued that the reason that this 'rich arctic coastal area [was] lying unused for thousands of years' is because it was necessary to develop a maritime technology before any colonisation could take place and that environmental change or social pressures in the North Sea plain may have inspired this. Perhaps in a broadly similar way, the large-scale settlement of Scotland required changes in people's routines forcing them to adapt to a rather different environment. The hints of early mesolithic or late glacial activity may indicate occasional visits, or reconnaissance, and it is only with the later mesolithic that substantial settlement began.

Accounts of these early periods are sketchy. Much evidence eludes us, lost beneath the peat bogs that have grown since this period, for example. A particular problem is that sea levels have risen since this period (see chapter 2). Archaeologists assume that coastal resources were of great importance to mesolithic hunter-gatherers and must therefore recognise that many early coastal sites have been lost to the rising sea (18). As stated above, the earliest site is Cramond, on the south shores of the Firth of Forth immediately west of Edinburgh, which indicates settlement at 8500-8300 BC. It is interesting that the assemblage from Cramond is 'later' mesolithic or 'narrow blade' in type, not 'early', suggesting, that the early–late mesolithic divide commonly used in Britain may not be correctly dated yet in Scotland. After Cramond, the next earliest dates come from inland sites. Manor Bridge, near Peebles, is located on a rocky outcrop above the River Tweed, and dates to 8500-8000 BC (colour plate 3). Daer, discovered by Tam Ward through examination at the edge of a reservoir high in the Lanarkshire hills (19), seems to have been occupied at 8000-7500 BC. Given the stress on the importance of the coast in our accounts of mesolithic people, it is very interesting to note that quite early dates are coming from a site that would have been inland or high in the hills, seemingly indicating that the coast was not the sole focus of the people's interests and that the landscape was explored quite quickly. It may also be significant that, despite the historical tendency for mesolithic research to take place in the west of Scotland, all of the early dates are coming from the east: this may indicate a movement of people into Scotland from this direction. This is in contrast to many previous models that suggested that colonisation followed the rich western seaways.

In contrast to the evidence from the late glacial or early mesolithic, the late mesolithic settlement of Scotland appears to have been quite widespread, and sites radiocarbon dated to this period are common. Finds of small, narrow blade microliths are also very common, and it is clear that in some regions hunter-gatherers were making extensive use of the resources of the Scottish landscape: the greater number of sites increases the range of questions archaeologists ask. Sites on both the east and west coast date to the centuries following 7500 BC. Kinloch on the island of Rùm is a large lithic scatter, with ephemeral structural evidence, excavated by Caroline Wickham-Jones. The area saw repeated hunter-gatherer activity over a very long time period. Over 100,000 lithics were recovered from the site, showing people using flint as well as a local material found only on Rùm – bloodstone. Most of the microliths are 'narrow blade' in type, with scalene triangle shapes being important. The site clearly shows people using boats quite routinely to access the island. On the east coast the site of Fife Ness, Fife, is much smaller and seems to have been only occupied once or possibly twice at about 7500 BC. The site has a small windbreak, surrounding an occupation soil and a few pits. Stone tools include small, narrow blade microliths – in particular a kind known as 'crescents'. It is interesting to note that these two broadly contemporary sites have different microliths. As the discussion has demonstrated, archaeologists have often considered the form of microliths to be an indicator of the age of the site. In some cases this is clearly the case, but there is much that is not understood about microliths. Are the differences between Kinloch and Fife Ness to do with the function of the sites? Or is it that these are evidence of different communities of hunter-gatherers who used different tool types? At present it is hard to be sure.

After these early dates, finds of mesolithic materials in Scotland are much more common. As noted above, the end of the mesolithic is very difficult to define. In Scotland the arrival of the neolithic is very controversial, with some writers suggesting that the transition to farming happened slowly, with mesolithic communities choosing to adopt agriculture. Others have suggested that colonisation was important. Regardless of the mechanism, changes seem to take place in the centuries following 4000 BC. In the east, the agricultural heartlands of Scotland, a large timber hall containing lots of cereals at Balbridie was burnt down between 3780-3640 BC. Pits from Dubton Farm near Brechin containing very similar crops date to 3940-3650 BC. These sites, and others, suggest the presence of successful agriculture early in the fourth millennium. Dates from a complex of pits containing pottery at Deskford, Banffshire, of 4200-3950 BC are the earliest dates for the new neolithic items in the region. On the west coast, Alison Sheridan of the National Museums of Scotland has argued for the clear influence of French farmers on the design of a pot and tomb from Achnacreebeag, Argyll, at around 4300-4000 BC. At the same date some of the mesolithic shell middens in the area fall out of use. Something, then, is clearly happening in and around 4000 BC. Be it colonisation by groups of incoming farmers or indigenous adoption of agriculture, or, most likely, a mixture of the two, the scale of the changes provides a useful point at which to draw this account of the mesolithic to a close.

So, how best to define the mesolithic period in Scotland? One could argue that the mesolithic in Scotland is a time when the country was occupied by hunter-gatherers at the end of, and after, the last Ice Age. This may date back as far as 11000 BC, although technically these people might be described as palaeolithic, not mesolithic highlighting the rather arbitrary nature of the terminology. In any case, this evidence is contentious and limited and, even if late glacial occupation did take place, there is little opportunity to look at their lives in much detail. Setting the late glacial evidence aside, one could argue that the mesolithic period broadly lies between around 9600 BC – a time following the initial rapid warming at the end of the Ice Age – and about 4000 BC, when new technologies, especially farming, make an appearance. The earliest solid evidence is about 8500 BC, although some aspects of stone-tool technologies imply some small-scale activity before this date. Most of what I will say in detail about hunter-gatherer lives therefore postdates about 8500 BC, but it will sometimes be possible to highlight earlier routines.

The focus of this book is therefore the hunter-gatherers who lived in the varied wooded landscapes of Scotland in the years from roughly 8500 BC to around 4000 BC. It is important to take stock of the length of time encompassed by the mesolithic in Scotland: there is clear evidence that humans have lived in Scotland since 8500 BC. People were hunters and gatherers for 4,500 of the 10,500 years since that date. Just by virtue of the length of time involved, hunter-gatherer lives are of considerable importance to the stories associated with the Scottish landscape.

CHANGE IN THE MESOLITHIC

I have stressed that the mesolithic is not the same from start to finish and highlighted some of the distinctions between early and late mesolithic stone tools, as well as late glacial groups. As discussed in chapter 2, the mesolithic period sees very significant changes in the Scottish landscape at a number of different timescales, many of which must have had important implications for the character of settlement. In fact, change within the mesolithic is increasingly well recognised, even if the reasons for this are not at all clear, and it would not be appropriate to assume that environmental changes drove all changes in hunter-gatherer communities.

For example, recent years have seen major archaeological projects focus on the mesolithic settlement of the southern Hebridean islands, especially Oronsay, Colonsay, Islay and Jura. These areas are now probably the best understood of all Scottish mesolithic landscapes – but are still controversial. Steve Mithen directed much of the research on Colonsay and Islay. The Southern Hebrides Mesolithic Project was able to show hunter-gatherers living on Colonsay, Islay and also Jura from around 7000 BC. There was evidence for large-scale exploitation of plant food as well as hunting, and it was argued that these were foragers utilising a wide range of different resources. The striking feature for this discussion is that there was a gap in the dates for activity from around 5700 BC down to just before 4000 BC. This is very interesting because a sequence of dates from shell middens on the tiny island of Oronsay fits almost exactly into this gap: superficially the dates seem to imply a shift of settlement from Colonsay, Islay and Jura to Oronsay. This is made even more interesting by the fact that the sites on Oronsay show communities heavily, if not exclusively, reliant on marine resources (fish, shellfish and sea mammals) rather than terrestrial resources.

Mithen identifies three possibilities to explain the evidence. Firstly, it is possible that hunter-gatherers changed their economic strategies, gave up exploiting the resources of Islay, Colonsay and Jura and moved to Oronsay, where they lived all the year round exploiting marine resources. Secondly, hunter-gatherers abandoned their long established hunting and gathering grounds and moved to the mainland, or Mull. They continued to be very mobile and visited Oronsay as part of their seasonal patterns of movement around the islands. The final possibility is that the evidence is just a biased sample of dates and sites, and has no historical significance: this seems unlikely and the choice is probably between the first two explanations. Regardless of which of these is true, the southern Hebrides shows clear evidence for a significant change during the mesolithic, and one that is not currently reflected in our chronological terminology. Other writers have argued that the final part of the mesolithic sees a heavy focus on the use of maritime resources, and that microliths actually fall out of use before the end of the period. These are controversial arguments but again imply the potential significance of change within the mesolithic. More recently Chantal Conneller and others have highlighted changes in the nature of the burial evidence within the British mesolithic, with the use of caves for the disposal of the dead in south-western Britain appearing to end in the centuries following 6000 BC.

Put simply, crude archaeological divisions of time do not adequately reflect the dynamism of mesolithic communities, and identifications of changes in stone tools do not appear to bear any straightforward relationship to wider changes in society. One way to resolve this problem would be to try subdividing and subdividing the period, with more and more names reflecting increasingly precise periods of time. I'm not convinced that this is the most helpful approach, as the data does not have enough coherency. Instead, I think we should simply recognise that the mesolithic (or the early or late mesolithic) is a very rudimentary label for a period of time in which hunter-gatherers did lots of different things.

RESOLUTION

I have been talking about dates in broad terms. Cramond, for example, is dated to 8500–8300 BC, a 200-year period. It is important to be clear about what this means. It would be easy to think that 8500–8300 means that the site was occupied from 8500 to 8300 BC, but this would be wrong. Radiocarbon dates, and their calibrated equivalents, express a range of time within which the date lies: 8500–8300 BC means that the site dates to some point (or points) within that 200-year period. Assuming that a human generation for hunter-gatherer communities is about 20 years (many hunter-gatherers have short life expectancies and marry young), then 200 years is ten generations: from a person back to their great-great-great-great-great-great-great-great-grandparents. And all we can do with Cramond is say that the site fits somewhere into these ten generations. This is not very precise. Yet Cramond is a well dated site; some of the artefacts we have discussed fit into a time period measured in the thousands of years. I raise this point not to despair at our inability to accurately date mesolithic sites, but to highlight crucial issues of resolution. The mesolithic as a term masks lots of variation over time, and most of the time we are lucky if we can fit a site into a 200-year time period. It isn't likely that people did precisely the same things for all that time; variations in the environment, climate and other changes will all have been important.

Whilst at the one level the archaeology of the mesolithic must work at broad timescales and have difficulties fitting sites into an exact chronological framework, it is also full of individual moments from the past: the moments at which a stone flake was struck from a core, with the core, the flake, and the debris associated with its manufacture all surviving in the archaeological record, very literally set in stone. Decisions to dump material on a shell midden, or to organise space around a central hearth lie behind the creation of the material studied today: mesolithic actions and episodes must be at the heart of any analyses.

To my mind the best way of reconciling this is to think about mesolithic lives in terms of fragments, collages and impressions. One can never be sure exactly what happened, or when. But what I can offer are fragmentary accounts of moments of mesolithic lives. It is quite possible that impressions from different sites will be contradictory. This may be because the interpretations are wrong; it may be that things had changed in the mesolithic; or it may be that the site has more than one story to tell about aspects of people's lives. My aim in this book, therefore, is to present a series of accounts of overlapping, fragmented moments of mesolithic lives and experiences.

REVIEW

This chapter has worked at very large temporal and spatial scales, in order to sketch some of the limits of the book. I have demonstrated how the human settlement of Scotland must be seen in a wider context, and how changing landscapes and environments may have played their part in the rhythms of human settlement. Despite hints of earlier settlement, the majority of the evidence from Scotland probably post-dates $c.8500$ BC and lies before 4000 BC. This 4,500-year period is the subject of the rest of the book. The chronological focus is coarse; and the communities discussed were diverse: I think of the book as being collage-like, or even impressionist, in its construction of these lives.

FURTHER READING

More detail of the development and refinement of radiocarbon dating can be found in Renfrew and Bahn (1996) and also at www.c14dating.com. General accounts of Britain at the end of the Ice Age and the start of the Holocene can be found in Barton (1999) and Mithen (1999). Discussions of the late glacial and early mesolithic in Scotland can be found in Ballin and Saville (2003), Bonsall (1988), Bjerck (1995), Finlayson (1999), Finlayson and Edwards (1997), Morrison and Bonsall (1990) and Smith (1992). Details of some of the excavated sites are found in Coles (1971), Wickham-Jones (1990) and Wickham-Jones and Dalland (1998). Mithen (2000, with further references) discusses the relationship between the southern Hebrides and Oronsay dates.

Ballin, T.B. and Saville, A. 2003. 'An Ahrensburgian-type tanged point from Shieldaig, Wester Ross, Scotland, and its implications' in *Oxford Journal of Archaeology* 22(2): pp.115-131

Barton, N. 1999. 'The Late glacial or Late and Final Upper Palaeolithic colonization of Britain' in J. Hunter and I.B.M. Ralston (eds) *The Archaeology of Britain: an introduction from the Upper Palaeolithic to the Industrial Revolution*, pp.13-34. (London: Routledge)

Bjerck, H.B. 1995. 'The North Sea Continent and the Pioneer settlement of Norway' in A. Fischer (ed.) *Man and the Sea in the Mesolithic*, pp.131-144. (Oxford: Oxbow Monograph 53)

Bonsall, C. 1988. 'Morton and Lussa Wood, the case for early Flandrian settlement of Scotland: comment on Myers' in *Scottish Archaeological Review* 5: 30-33

Coles, J.M. 1971. 'The Early Settlement of Scotland: Excavations at Morton, Fife' in *Proceedings of the Prehistoric Society* 37: pp.284-366

Edwards, K.J. and Ralston, I.B.M. (eds) 1997. *Scotland, environment and archaeology 8000 BC-AD 1000*. (Chichester)

Finlayson, B. 1999. 'Understanding the Initial Colonisation of Scotland' in *Antiquity* 73: pp.879-883

Finlayson, B. and Edwards, K. 1997. 'The Mesolithic' in K. Edwards and I.B.M. Ralston (eds) *Scotland: environment and Archaeology 8000BC-AD1000*, pp.109-125. (Edinburgh: John Wiley & Sons)

Mithen, S.J. 2000. 'Mesolithic sedentism on Oronsay: chronological evidence from adjacent islands in the southern Hebrides' in *Antiquity* 74: pp.298-304

Morrison, A. and Bonsall, C. 1989. 'The Early Post Glacial Settlement of Scotland: a review' in C. Bonsall (ed.) *The Mesolithic in Europe*, pp.134-142. (Edinburgh: John Donald)

Renfrew, C. and Bahn, P. 1996. *Archaeology: theories, methods and practice*. (London: Thames & Hudson)

Smith, C. 1992. *Late Stone Age Hunters of the British Isles*. (London: Routledge)

Wickham-Jones, C.R. 1990. *Rhum: Mesolithic and later sites at Kinloch, excavations 1984- 86*. (Edinburgh: Society of Antiquaries of Scotland Monograph)

Wickham-Jones, C.R. and Dalland, M. 1998. 'A small mesolithic site at Fife Ness, Fife, Scotland'. *Internet Archaeology* 5: http://intarch.ac.uk/journal/issue5/wickham_index. html

See also: http://www.c14dating.com

AN INTERJECTION

You mentioned the difference between radiocarbon and calendar dates. What's the basis for this?

Radiocarbon dating is based on radioactive decay of a carbon isotope (carbon 14, hence C14 dating) contained in all living organisms. On the death of an organism its carbon intake ceases, and the radioactive decay begins. By measuring the extent of decay of the minute amounts of this isotope present in an archaeological material, we can work out roughly how long ago the material died. These estimates are expressed as years before present (bp/BP which actually means 1950) and with a statistical margin of error. For example, an archaeologist might discover some burnt hazelnuts on a site. A hazelnut could be sent off for dating and return a date of 9150±45 bp. The date would mean that the hazelnuts had stopped taking in carbon isotopes from the atmosphere 9150 plus or minus 45 years before 1950. Therefore, assuming there was no reason to suspect that material of different ages had become mixed together, the archaeologist might assume that the site was of the same age: 7200 BC.

But there is a slight problem. It was initially assumed that radiocarbon dates were the same as calendar dates. Unfortunately, due to variation in the amount of cosmic radiation over time there have been fluctuations in the formation of C14, and radiocarbon and calendar years can vary significantly. In order to convert radiocarbon dates into calendar years, it is necessary to calibrate the raw radiocarbon age. This has been done by establishing the radiocarbon ages of items of known calendar ages, using the annual growth patterns of tree rings to establish an absolute chronology. Computer programmes carry out calibration and the results are expressed as a range. Sometimes the differences between radiocarbon and calendar dates can be very large. For example, our radiocarbon date of 9150±45 bp calibrates at 8530-8260 BC in calendar years, over 1,000 years older than we might have thought.

OK. I think I'm getting this. But I've been looking at the books and they seem to use all kinds of dates and abbreviations for them. It's all a bit confusing. Am I getting something wrong?

No, you're not getting anything wrong. It is confusing. Archaeologists are very vague and inconsistent about what kind of date they mean when discussing the mesolithic. Some, especially those interested in the environment, tend to use uncalibrated radiocarbon years; others use calibrated calendar years. This can make things very confusing. There are abbreviations: in general BP means before present and BC before Christ. Sometimes a convention is used where the use of lower case (bp/bc) means that the date is uncalibrated (i.e. is a radiocarbon age not a calendar age). This isn't always the case though, and you need to take care when reading.

Why are you using calendar dates?

There are good arguments for the use of either kind of date: the basis for calibration changes over time, and therefore the dates I give in this book may be changed slightly over the next 10 -15 years. That said, I find calendar years give me a better sense of timescale, and in a book on mesolithic lives that seemed crucial.

2

THE CHANGING LANDSCAPE

Sometime between 6000 and 5750 BC a huge underwater rock slip off the Norwegian coast (the Støregga rock slip) displaced an enormous body of water. This displaced water formed a large tsunami, which raced across the North Sea and hit the coasts of eastern Scotland. Exactly how high the wave was is not known, but David Smith, a specialist in coastal geomorphology from Coventry University, suggests that:

> ... the Støregga slide was a spectacular event along the coast ... flooding may have extended kilometres inland in low-lying estuarine areas, and the erosion of coastal spits and bars would have been notable.
> Smith, D.E. 2002. 'The Støregga Disaster'. *Current Archaeology* 179 (May 2002): 468-471, p.470

In the light of the tsunami of December 2004, it hardly needs emphasising that an event of this kind must have been devastating for wildlife and vegetation in the area. Mesolithic people may have been in the area at the time: some writers have suggested that there is evidence of occupied mesolithic sites hit by the wave. At Castle Street, Inverness, for example, sands deposited by the tsunami lie immediately above mesolithic archaeology. As long ago as 1886 Hutcheson commented that a shell midden at Broughty Ferry, near Dundee, showed evidence for being disturbed by an exceptional tide. However, it is far from clear whether the sites at Inverness or Broughty Ferry were actually in use at the time the wave hit: such sites are likely to have been occupied only seasonally, and indeed may have not been visited for generations due to changes in patterns of movement. In any case, Caroline Wickham-Jones has pointed out that because mesolithic structures are generally lightweight, they are likely to have been completely destroyed by such a wave rather than buried intact, and that therefore the search for 'squashed mesolithic people' is likely to be fruitless. Notwithstanding this, the wave must have been a key feature in people's lives: returning to familiar landscapes to find them waterlogged, eroded or removed.

The Støregga tsunami is a striking example of one of the features of the world of mesolithic hunter-gatherers in Scotland. The mesolithic landscape of Scotland was dynamic and unstable, changing at a variety of timescales. Today most people acknowledge the importance of climate change, noting the impact of global warming on sea level rise and on the timing of the seasons. The causes of these changes are a source of much debate. Many people recognise human activity as at least a contributing factor, if not the dominant process involved. Others argue that climate change in the Holocene is constant and complicated, and that therefore establishing the influence of human activity is a formidably complex task. This is not the place for an extensive discussion of these issues, but it is interesting to note that mesolithic communities had to deal with changing sea levels, weather patterns and migrations of flora and fauna as well as dramatic short-term events such as tsunamis. In fact, the landscape of the mesolithic was much more dynamic than anything we are familiar with today. Most likely, mesolithic communities recognised these changes, and interpreted the reasons for these changes in varied ways. The contemporary concern with climate change is therefore not an exclusively modern phenomenon.

This chapter explores the changing landscapes of the mesolithic in Scotland, paying particular attention to the scales at which these changes took place – how many of these processes were visible to mesolithic people? I outline, in turn, climate change, sea level change, changes in flora and fauna, and close with a discussion of the implications of these changes.

CLIMATE CHANGE

For many years environmental scientists offered a straightforward story of climate change since the end of the last Ice Age. Climate gradually ameliorated (improved), enabling the slow migration of plant and animal communities back into the British Isles. Scientists divided the postglacial into periods (20) of which the main periods of interest in a mesolithic context are the Boreal and Atlantic. The Boreal, a warm, dry period, incorporated the 'climatic optimum', the culmination of the gradual postglacial warming, and a time when average temperatures in Britain were higher than they are today. The Boreal saw woodland cover Britain, initially represented by birch but becoming fuller over time. Then a change in climate took place, with the cooler, wetter more oceanic conditions of the Atlantic period, connected by some to sea level rise (see below). This period saw closed-canopy 'climax' woodland cover the landscape: the supposed stable, natural 'primeval' forest of north-west Europe. The dominant tree types through most of northern Britain were believed to be oak and hazel, except in the extreme north and the Highlands (a major exception in a Scottish context). The end of the mesolithic, at broadly 4000 BC, coincides with a change to a drier climate and the more marked influence of people on woodland, with the appearance of clearings, evidence of domesticated plants, and possible evidence for soil erosion seemingly indicating the presence of farming as a transformation of the wildwood, at least at small scales.

This model of gradual amelioration giving way to Boreal (and light) woodlands followed by Atlantic (and dense) woodlands, has been of considerable importance in structuring understandings of mesolithic climates, woodlands, and human behaviour. It is also, unfortunately, somewhat misleading. New data has transformed models of Holocene climate, most importantly through the recognition of variation over time; climatic or environmental changes take place rapidly, on a regional basis. For example climatic improvement at the beginning of the Holocene was extraordinarily rapid, with temperatures greater than those of today reached within decades, or centuries at the most, from the end of the Younger Dryas. The slow appearance of trees after this rapid warming, often taken as evidence for slow amelioration, simply reflected the great distances theses species had to migrate from warmer and more clement environments.

The reasons for the rapidity of the climate changes are still controversial, but one key factor is the importance of the Gulf Stream to the British climate. The Gulf Stream brings a supply of warm water to western Scottish shores and is responsible for the surprising warmth of the British Isles, given its northerly location: most famously, for the ability of introduced palm trees to survive and prosper in north-west Scotland. Variation in the flow of the Gulf Stream over time therefore has a considerable influence on climate, as highlighted dramatically in the recent film *The Day After Tomorrow*, where changes in the Gulf Stream led to a catastrophic freezing event. Artistic licence aside, it is clear that, throughout the Holocene, changes in North Atlantic circulation, especially in the polar regions, have greatly affected the supplies of warm water to these shores. A good example of this, and a wonderful illustration of the instability of Holocene climate (and the problems with the traditional, static models) is the so-called '8200 cal BP event'. In the centuries surrounding approximately 6200 BC (so 8200 BP), changes in the structure of the North American Ice Sheet (which was still melting away after the Ice Age) led to dramatic changes in North Atlantic circulation. The consequences over a 200-400-year period in northern Europe were dramatic. In Norway temperature dropped by 1-3°c a year, the climate became drier and the tree line dropped. In Germany tree rings show a decline of growth of over one third for this period. In Greenland temperature fell by 6±2°c. The exact implications of the '8200 event' in Scotland are not known, but they seem must have been significant. A cold period of 200-400 years is going to have had major implications for the decisions made by mobile hunter-gatherers reliant on natural resources. Other examples of changes in climate change exist; another cold snap, for example, is recorded for *c*.4500-4400 BC.

The dynamism of the climate of Holocene Scotland is striking, but many of the details of these changes and their impacts in particular regions are contentious; the study of ancient climates is a rapidly developing and changing field. The timescales at which these events took place, and the ways in which people may have negotiated them, are discussed at the end of this chapter.

TURNING TIDES

Perhaps the most immediately dramatic of the natural processes to affect the Scottish landscape since the end of the last Ice Age is sea level change. Over the years changes in

Period	Inferred Climate	Approximate age C14 bp uncal.	Approx age cal BC
Pre-Boreal	cool-dry	10000 – 9500	9600/9300 – 9000/8800
Boreal	warm-dry	9500 – 7000	9000/8800 – 6000/5800
Atlantic	warm-wet	7000 – 5000	6000/5800 – 3900/3700
Sub-Boreal	warm-dry	5000 – 2500	3900/3700 – 780/540
Sub-Atlantic	cool-wet	2500 – present	780/540 – present

20 Traditional periodic division of climate in the Holocene. 'C14 bp uncal' means radiocarbon years

the relative amounts of water held in ice, and the effect of the ice weighing down the land, have led to significant variation in the relative height of the sea. At times these sea levels have been stable enough to cut cliffs, or deposit sediments – landscape features now left as fossils.

Postglacial sea level changes arose from the interplay of absolute sea level change (glacio-eustasy), the rebound of the landmass after the removal of glaciers (glacio-isostasy) and the depression of the ocean floors under the weight of the extra water (hydro-isostasy). Glacio-eustasy is the absolute change in global sea level caused by ice-melt. In the Ice Age vast amounts of water were caught up in the varied ice fields, and as this slowly melted sea level rose. The ice-sheets were heavy enough to depress the land surfaces beneath them. Glacio-isostasy describes the continuing steady rise of the landmass of Scotland after the glacier's weight was removed. Uplift has not been even; the area of maximum uplift is Rannoch Moor, centre of the ice formations in the last glaciation (*21*). Away from here the amount of uplift decreases relatively steadily. Uplift was quickest early in the Holocene, slowing over time and it still continues, albeit very slowly, in many areas of Scotland. Hydro-isostasy describes the depression of the sea floor caused by the increased weight of water in the oceans. The interaction between these processes led to radically different sea levels during the mesolithic, and consequently a very different geography. Many of the local details of these changes are controversial, and a simplified account is given here.

Sea level at the beginning of the Holocene was high but by *c.*9000 BC isostatic uplift began to be important. As isostatic uplift continued, relative sea level fell, with some fossil beach features being formed below present sea level. This continued until approximately 7500-7300 BC, the lowest sea level in the Postglacial. As uplift slowed, sea level rise through melt-waters became the most important process and a long 'transgressive' episode began (transgression refers to the sea encroaching on the land). Due to the uneven rate at which the land was bouncing back up from the weight of the ice this transgression (the Main Post Glacial Transgression – MPGT) culminated at different times in different places, and differences in the pace of rebound mean that these shorelines are now at different heights. In the Firth of Forth for example, the MPGT shoreline is about 15m above present sea level, and indicates the sea level at *c.*5700-5650 BC. On the north-west

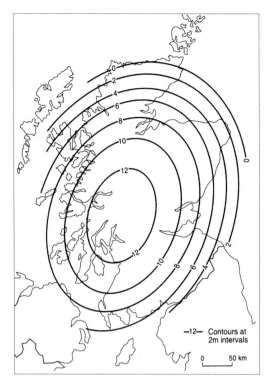

−12− Contours at
2m intervals

0   50 km

21 Isobases for Main Postglacial Shoreline.
Figures indicate height in metres above OD
of contemporary altitude of shoreline. *After
Ballantyne 2004 Fig 7 with modifications*

coast of Islay, when the transgression culminated at some stage after *c.*5800 BC the sea
was at about 5m above present sea level, separating the Rhins from the rest of Islay. In
contrast, at Philorth, Aberdeenshire, the transgression reached its maximum at around
5000 BC and the MPGT lies only 1.5m above the present shore.

Regardless of the details these examples demonstrate that from 7500-7300 BC through
to about 5000 BC, when the North American and Scandinavian ice-sheets were gone
and absolute sea level stabilised, sea levels around Scotland were rising. After about
5000 BC sea level has been more stable, and slowly some ancient coastlines have been
isostatically lifted upwards away from the current shore creating 'raised beaches'. In other
areas uplift has never been an important phenomenon, and sea level rise has inundated
ancient coastlines: for example Orkney and the Western Isles (see *18* and *19*). The extent
of sea level change reminds us again of how different Scotland would have appeared.
At the height of the transgression in the Forth the north and south of Scotland were
connected by a land bridge only 12km wide.

The changes in sea level since the end of the last Ice Age also have very important
implications for understandings of mesolithic communities. Coastal resources seem to
have been important for mesolithic subsistence, and many scholars have presumed that
for at least part of the year mesolithic groups made use of coastal sites. Considering this
in terms of sea level change highlights dramatic biases. For the period from 9000 BC
through to 7500-7300 BC sea levels fell, and coastal sites would slowly have moved further
and further out into what is now the sea. The transgressing sea is likely to have buried or

destroyed these sites as it made its way inland (and on the east coast, the tsunami of 6000-5750 may have destroyed more). By approximately 6000-5800 BC in some areas uplift began to lift small parts of the mesolithic coastline away from the waves, and by c.5000 BC the rate of transgression had slowed. Nevertheless steady coastal erosion continues to remove ancient coastlines. This implies that for much of the mesolithic period in Scotland coastal sites are now buried at sea, or destroyed by transgressing waves. In some areas uplift preserves mesolithic coastlines from the later part of the period – depending on the location, some time from c.6000-5000 BC. Understanding the mesolithic use of the coasts of Scotland is therefore reliant on a sample of, at best, 2000 years at the end of the mesolithic, and does not cover all of the country. It is very difficult to determine whether patterns of land use identified for the later part of the period are appropriate for the early part. There is a wide range of evidence, for example, from the middens on Oronsay to suggest that marine resources were of considerable importance around 5000-4000 BC. Is this picture representative of the whole of the mesolithic? It is difficult to tell, because it is only really for this late period that preserved coastlines enable the examination of these questions.

But these changes are not a reason to despair. In a wider British context any preservation of mesolithic sea levels is rare and the fragments of these landscapes uplifted in Scotland (and some of the northeastern parts of Ireland) are therefore vitally important. It is a pity that the sample is not larger, but at least there is something. As well as finding middens, flint scatters and other archaeological sites on top of raised beaches, lifted away from the waves, the MPGT has left other important pieces of evidence.

In the large estuaries of eastern Scotland, for example, the transgressing sea deposited large amounts of fine sediment. These deposits, now known as carse clays, have formed a good environment for preserving organic artefacts such as bone, antler or even wood. The carse clays were extensively drained for agriculture in the nineteenth and early twentieth centuries and in this process a number of important mesolithic artefacts were discovered (22-25). At Meiklewood, Stirling, for example, a mattock, made out of a perforated antler tine, dates to about 5000-4580 BC, and was perhaps deposited or lost just as relative sea levels began to fall in this area (22). Other finds include a fine biserial (barbs on both sides) harpoon from the Forth at Carriden, Falkirk, dating to 5060-4770 BC (23). Perhaps most dramatically, some finds of mesolithic artefacts were made in conjunction with the skeletons of whales. It has often been assumed that these finds demonstrate the exploitation of chance strandings, although this assumption may simply demonstrate preconceptions about mesolithic activity. Whale hunting in the mesolithic is known in Scandinavia and the presence of mesolithic finds on the Outer Hebrides and Northern Isles is testimony to skilled sea crossings. Sea passage and the skills associated with it were central to some people's lives in the mesolithic.

On the west coast the changing sea levels have preserved a very different kind of evidence. As noted above, whilst the encroaching seas moved inland they destroyed earlier evidence of mesolithic settlement, with waves pounding into light post-holes and small flint scatters. Some artefacts resulting from this destruction must have laid on the beaches before being finally eroded away. In some areas of western Scotland, and also in north-east

Ireland, some of the find spots of these artefacts were isostatically uplifted before they could be completely destroyed. The flints therefore became part of raised beach deposits. These 'raised beach' flint scatters are problematic archaeological resources. The stone tools are battered and rolled from wave action, and often altered by chemical processes ('patinated' and a ghostly white in colour) as well. It is sometimes very difficult to be certain whether a particular piece is worked or not. The finds also lack any real context – any remains of structures are gone and it is impossible to gauge how much the pieces have moved before they were deposited by the waves, or how many different sites have been mixed together. Nevertheless these pieces have played an important part in the history of mesolithic studies in Scotland (and Ireland) and they should not be neglected.

The implications of sea level change reach beyond the immediate concerns of locating artefacts and understanding the importance of the coast – although the importance of these issues should be stressed. The changes in sea level have fundamental effects on the character of north-west European geography; at a very basic level it was during the mesolithic period that Britain became cut off from the rest of continent. Bryony Coles, for example, has recently stressed that the changing geography of north-west Europe provided not just a link between places (Britain and the continent), but a viable place to live in itself. She has offered detailed reconstructions of the region, noting the importance of 'Doggerland, so-named after Doggerbank' (*18*). It is fascinating that occasional finds of archaeological material have been made from under the North Sea. As noted in the last chapter, it is also in this radically different landscape context that we must consider the early evidence of human settlement in Scotland.

Finally, it is important to consider the paces of change in sea level. A generalised account like this stresses the slow playing out of processes, but it is clear that the rates of sea level change varied greatly. Even slow changes in sea level might have rapid local manifestations depending on topography. It might take years for the sea to surmount a small cliff, but once it did a low lying area could rapidly be inundated. Recent work on Islay offers some detail in this context. Research by Sue and Alastair Dawson suggests that at one time sea level changes may have been as rapid as 6.5m in 100 years, a fantastically rapid rate of increase and one that must have been recognised by mesolithic communities (clearly 6.5m per 100 years was not sustained throughout the mesolithic). Even more dramatically it is proposed that the sudden emptying of an ice-dammed lake from the North American ice sheet around 7500-7000 BC led to a worldwide sea level rise of 0.25-0.50m in 48 hours.

Changes in the sea level, then, during and since the mesolithic period, are of vital importance to understanding hunter-gatherer lives in Scotland. The end of this chapter considers the ways in which hunter-gatherers may have been affected by these processes, but it is important to note that the rhythms and scales of these changes were sometimes dramatic.

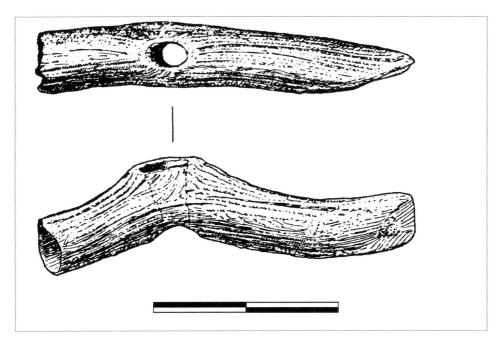

22 Antler beam mattock from Meiklewood, Stirling. Reproduced at 1:2. *After Lacaille 1954 Fig 65*

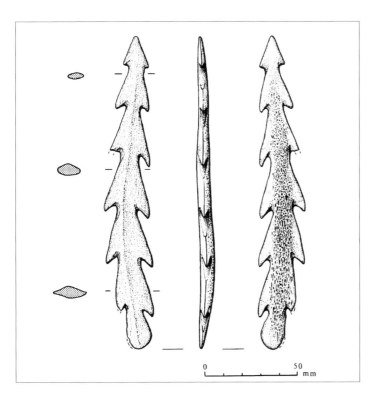

23 Barbed point, Carriden, Falkirk. Reproduced at 1:2. *Saville 2004 Fig 10.11. Drawing by Marion O'Neill, reproduced with kind permission of Alan Saville and the Society of Antiquaries of Scotland*

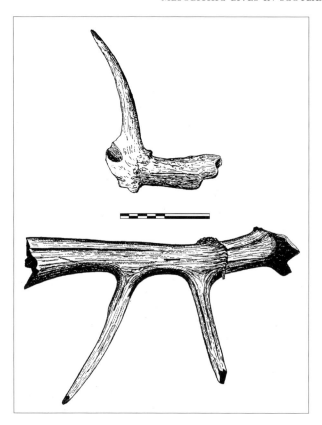

24 Antler artefacts, possibly
borers, from carse clays
of the Forth. Upper from
Causewayhead, lower from
Stirling Bridge. Reproduced at
1:4. *After Lacaille 1954 Fig 65*

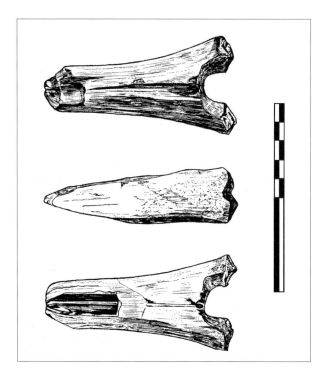

25 Fragmentary antler tool
supposedly from Grangemouth,
Firth of Forth. Reproduced at
1:2. *After Lacaille 1954 Fig 66*

CHANGES IN THE LAND

At the end of the last Ice Age Scotland was a bare landscape of rock and poorly developed soils with lichens and some hardy shrubs and plants. After the Loch Lomond Stadial initial postglacial conditions were herb- and shrub-dominated. Slowly over time, migrations of plant communities created a great variety of different woodland types: and it is worth stressing that the early prehistoric landscape of Scotland was a wooded landscape; the bare moors of today's picture postcards are the product of a complex interplay between human activity and natural processes, but humans were central to creating and maintaining the open landscape of Scotland. The broad outlines of the changing Scottish woodlands are reasonably well understood, whilst many details remain rather obscure. This chapter provides an overview of the histories of woodlands in Scotland, before the characteristics of woodlands and the experience of living in woodland are discussed in more detail in chapter 4.

The reconstruction of Scottish woodlands is mainly reliant on the analysis of ancient pollen – the science of palynology. Pollen is robust, especially if deposited in wet conditions: a lake or a bog, for example. Over the years pollen accumulates in these deposits, each year adding a new fall of material, the bog therefore contains a history of the surrounding woodlands over time. Elongated vertical samples, or cores, of this material are taken, and the analysis of the changing representation of pollen grains over time thus enables the history of the immediate environment surrounding the wet deposit to be read. In turn, and with all due care to issues of pollen representation and movement, wider models of environmental change can be offered.

Birch was a rapid colonising tree, appearing initially in the south at *c*.9500 BC and over most of Scotland by *c*.9000 BC, its dramatic speed of spread across the country suggesting few competitive species. Hazel soon followed, present in most locations by 8500-8000 BC. These early birch woods with some hazel are an interesting example of one of the characteristics of the woods of early Holocene Scotland. Most present-day birch woods tend to flourish at high altitudes and in cold locations, whereas in the early Holocene, because of different competitive interactions to today, such woods existed in lowland areas at much greater ranges of temperature. These woods therefore have no immediate analogue – it is not possible to point at a woodland anywhere in the world today (for example see *colour plate 4*) and say that the woodlands of early Holocene Scotland were like *that*. This has important implications for use of environmental analogies in understanding mesolithic communities.

Other slower migrating trees appeared around and after *c*.8000 BC with the initial appearance of oak and elm being broadly contemporary, although their rates of spread varied. Oak migrates very slowly, and its northern movement was greatly hampered by the Grampian mountains: it reached Aberdeenshire by about 5000-4750 BC. Elm was a slightly quicker mover than oak, and may have been geographically widespread by about 7500 BC; however, away from the south and south-east it was never very common. Pine (*26*) is believed to have spread from the north-west, or possibly Ireland, expanding through the Highlands from *c*.6500-5800 BC and only reaching the extreme northern mainland much later in prehistory.

26 Scots Pine, Balgavies Loch. © G. Warren

Regional variations in the character of woodlands were significant. Colour plate 5 offers a generalised distribution of woodland types at the end of the mesolithic. The Southern Uplands, Central Belt and southern slopes of the Highlands, especially in the east, were dominated by oak woodland with elm and hazel, and with greater proportions of birch and hazel in the uplands. Further north and east, through Aberdeenshire and the fertile plains of the Moray Firth, elm was not significant in an oak and hazel woodland. This mixed hazel and oak woodland was also found throughout the western seaways as far as Skye. The Highlands proper were dominated by pine with birch, and some of the highest areas were treeless. In the north the plains of Caithness and Sutherland as well as the Outer Hebridean, Orkney and Shetland isles have birch scrub only. These broad distinctions between the woodlands of areas are important, but it must be stressed that this is only the situation at the end of the mesolithic. For example, as noted above, oak may not have been important in Aberdeenshire until after *c.*5000 BC. It is also important to note the changes in the character of the woodlands of particular areas of Scotland over time. This includes not just species, but the complete dynamics of ecosystems. For example, Richard Tipping believes that woodland dynamics in northern Scotland shifted after about 7000 BC, leading to a greater prevalence of natural fires.

Such overviews do not do justice to complex local manifestations of woodland types. These are greatly affected by local topographic conditions and soils as well as chance events such as wind throws caused by large storms. A good example is altitude. Different woodland communities are affected differentially by altitude – north of the Tay the oak and elm component of a mixed birch–hazel dominated woodland was very sharply limited by height. Woodlands changed character with height providing distinctive ecotones. Alder was significant in damp and boggy locations. The mesolithic woodlands of Scotland were not monolithic, but highly varied and complex spaces. As Richard Tipping states: 'By the later mesolithic period, woodland structure varied in many ways in space, at all spatial scales, and presented a variety of landscapes, extraordinarily diverse mosaics of difference woodlands and open ground, within which mesolithic communities operated.' (2004: 46). This diversity, and its distinction from many powerful cultural images of woodland, is a key theme.

These generalised comments give a broad sense of the characteristics of Scotland's mesolithic woodlands, and of the importance of diachronic change in the landscape. The critical point to stress is that the mesolithic experience of Scotland was of a woodland landscape. Indeed, at the largest of scales, the adaptation of postglacial hunting and gathering communities to the arrival of woodlands is one of the definitive features of the mesolithic. Woods are central to any understanding of mesolithic lives in Scotland.

It is, of course, also important to consider other changes in the land since the mesolithic. One of the most significant of these is that much of the Scottish landscape today is the product of management, especially drainage. The Scottish landscape in early prehistory would have been much wetter and boggier than it is at present. Such wetland landscapes may have been important to early prehistoric settlers in Europe as a whole; wetlands were environments that saw a large amount of hunter-gatherer activity, including seemingly deliberate votive deposits of material into watery contexts. In fact, a great many finds of mesolithic material in Scotland occurred near such boggy areas. A number of sites are known; for example, on and above the Ettrick and its tributary the Yarrow in the Scottish Borders. These include finds near old lochans, overlooking small lochs and scattered across a landscape described by Mason in 1931 as 'the bleak moorlands to the south and east of Selkirk … presenting the same features of bare hill tips broken here and there by little marshes or lochs'. In this regard, it is also important to note that, although the dates of peat formation in Scotland are controversial, extensive areas of peatland would have been rare in mesolithic Scotland.

This chapter has outlined broad-scale processes associated with the end of the Ice Age in Scotland – climatic change, sea level rise and fall, and the time-transgressive migration of plant communities. There also other processes that would have contributed to an ever changing landscape, even if they are often harder to reconstruct. A very striking example of this is the importance of earthquakes during the mesolithic period. As the Scottish landmass slowly uplifted from the weight of the ice, earthquakes were much more frequent than today. In the immediate postglacial period, these may have been up to magnitude 6.5-7.0 on the Richter scale; which today would be classified as strong earthquakes, which may cause a lot of damage. The British Geological Survey record the largest known earthquake in Britain as a quake of magnitude 6.1 which happened on 7 June 1931 with an epicentre at Dogger Bank. Tremors were felt in Britain, east Ireland, Holland, Belgium, parts of northern France and Germany and south-west Norway. The earthquake caused cliff collapse at Flamborough Head and Mundesley, Norfolk. Earthquakes of magnitude 6.5-7.0 were major events at a landscape level.

It is difficult to know how people reacted to such events, although in conjunction with all the other incidents of landscape change noted so far another example of instability may not have been a cause of much surprise. In the west of Scotland caves and rock shelters seem to have been an important settlement type for mesolithic communities – for

27 Waisted pebbles, interpreted as net sinkers, Selkirk Museum. Scale bar at 5cm intervals. Many other interpretations of these artefacts are possible and it is not clear that are genuinely of mesolithic date. © *G. Warren*

example at Ulva or Oban in the Inner Hebrides. Recent work carried out by Caroline Wickham-Jones and Karen Hardy in the Inner Sound of Skye has been trying to find ways of thinking about the importance of rock-falls in this kind of sites – earthquakes may have had a very immediate impact for settlement in a rock shelter (*colour plate 6*).

River systems may also have been an important source of change. River systems are inherently dynamic and given that many of Scotland's valleys contained large amounts of easily reworked glacially derived sediment, river profiles will have changed considerably during the Holocene, not least in association with sea level change. The complex geomorphic history of rivers and their associated landforms is still poorly understood, especially in the uplands, but episodes of downcutting (valley deepening caused by erosion of the stream bed) were common, especially in the early part of the period. Sedimentation, flooding and braiding river channels (where a rivers flows in a network of channels separated by small islands or bars) may all have been important processes, especially in terms of woodlands and settlement near rivers. Many lochs will have been slowly in-filled by sediments from rivers, changing their morphology and patterns of water movement (*colour plate 7*). The embanked, heavily managed and supposedly stable rivers of today are no analogue for those of prehistory.

RATES OF CHANGE

This sketch of some of the characteristics of the Scottish landscape is deliberately being drawn to evoke the dynamism, instability and change inherent in early Holocene Scotland.

This is a landscape rocked by earthquakes, struck by tidal waves, with seas rising 50cm in two days, and nearly four times the height of a person in a century. New tree types appear, transforming local ecological systems. A river floods, clearing a stand of birch and leaving room for alder to colonise. Small lakes or mires in old kettle holes (an ice wastage feature) slowly fill with sediment and eventually are choked. Climates change suddenly and dramatically. Of course, there were many periods of relative stability in the mesolithic landscape but the sense of dynamic change is overwhelming. In turn, this makes it ever more apparent that the term mesolithic is a very broad label, for a very diverse set of communities living in changing landscapes. I find it hard to expect the communities of the mesolithic to have continued doing the same thing through all of these changes.

I believe that this landscape dynamism also has important consequences for understanding mesolithic people. There are two issues here. The first concerns temporal resolution and the kinds of interpretations of the mesolithic that are possible; points that I have already raised, but are hopefully clearer now that the extent of landscape change is apparent. The second focuses on how mesolithic people negotiated these changes.

Trying to understand how hunter-gatherers made sense of changing environments is not straightforward. At the broadest of scales the loss of land to the rising sea has been connected to increased pressure on resources, territoriality and restrictions on mobility. It is hard to know how to assess these arguments, which seem inherently likely, but are constructed at a very generalised level. Some writers have even suggested that the final disappearance of Doggerland may have been implicated in the adoption of agriculture in the British Isles. At a similar broad level changes in microlith technology and settlement patterns in central and northern England have been connected to increasingly dense woodland. These arguments are particularly difficult in Scotland, where, as discussed in the following chapter, there are many reasons to suppose that the woodland was not dense and impenetrable, and in many places the composition of woodlands is not comparable to England anyway.

Another way in which instability affected mesolithic communities in the British Isles might be connected to the availability of predictable fishing runs. Many anthropologists have commented on the exceptional hunter-gatherer communities of coastal Northwest America. These groups of people live in large sedentary villages, have hereditary chiefs and large accumulations of wealth, the accretion and distribution of which forms a key part of social life. Their economy is based on the intensive exploitation of anadromous (migratory) fish, especially salmon. Many British mesolithic sites are located near important salmon rivers, especially in Scotland, and historical records suggest a similarly superabundant resource in recent years – over 125,000 fish a year were being caught on the Tweed in the early nineteenth century. However, there is little sign of the intensity of fishing found in America in the mesolithic of Scotland, with no evidence of specialised fishing tools, or large-scale processing for storage. Some simple coarse stone tools formed by removing two small notches from either side are known from the Tweed Valley (*27* and *colour plate 8*). Often interpreted as 'net sinkers' these artefacts, better described as waisted pebbles, are rather ambiguous as regards both function and date: they may be mesolithic, although this has not been demonstrated clearly, and many uses are possible; from weights in nets, use in a bolas or for stretching hide. Although biases, especially the poor preservation of bone, may be important in the absence of evidence for fishing, there are numerous reasons why a specialist salmon fishing economy should not have developed in Scotland, most of which come down to choice. One important factor may be that in the context of global instability of sea levels the runs of anadromous fish can be unpredictable in the short and medium term. Indeed, it is only with global stabilisation of sea levels after around 5000 BC that intensive fishing develops in the Americas. This medium-term instability in resource availability, recognised by mesolithic people, may therefore have been one reason to utilise a more generalised economy, in which salmon played a part, rather than one intensively reliant upon them. In this context the evidence for a greater reliance on migratory fish in Ireland is of considerable interest. Here, key sites such as Mount Sandel, on the River Bann, indicate the considerable role played by migratory salmon/trout and eel to mesolithic diets. It seems very likely that because of the impoverished terrestrial fauna of this island (with fewer large mammals available than in mainland Britain, including an important absence of red deer) mesolithic occupants of Ireland may have had less choice to avoid reliance on resources like salmon and eel.

These comments give some sense of the interaction between mesolithic life and large-scale environmental change in the British Isles, and, importantly, of the human decisions that negotiated these changes. All too often accounts of hunting and gathering communities present them as determined by environmental considerations, and leave too little room for choice. But these accounts are still frustratingly vague. Is it possible to draw any more intimate portraits of the ways in which environmental changes affected communities?

One way of thinking about this is to consider the long transgressive episode that lasted through so much of the mesolithic period. As discussed above, the paces of change in sea level varied, but at times transgressions could be rapid and must have been recognisable within the lifetime of individuals. At a more mundane level changes in the sea level must have been tied up with the loss or transformation of resources – good regions for the collection of cobble flint or particularly productive shellfish beds (which are closely related to the tides and particular microenvironments of rock or sand). Sea level change would have made subtle differences to intimate routines of movement around the landscape, as well as large-scale movements, for example breaching headlands and creating islands.

At the very least therefore, sea level changes would have been recognisable at the intergenerational level and stories about sea level change likely formed an important part of oral tradition. A grandparent might tell stories of their parent's camp, now beneath the sea, out beyond the low headland at the end of the bay. In this regard it is interesting that mesolithic communities appear to have made fairly routine use of boats in and around the shore (and possibly further out to sea: see chapter 5). At times it is likely that people were very literally sailing over the homes of their ancestors. The rolled and patinated flints of the raised beaches of the west of Scotland are also significant. On a number of sites on Jura, Colonsay and Islay these are found in small numbers in later flint scatters – implying that people had collected these recognisably human, but transformed, artefacts. The flints were possibly just a convenient source of raw material, but if we today can recognise the flints as worked it seems likely that skilled flint workers would also have done so. Such objects must have been a source of some debate – who had made these ghostly tools, some of which were of types no longer in use, and where had they come from or gone to?

Of course the details are obscure, but the particular interplay of human lives and changes in the landscape creates some very particular material encounters between people and the traces of past lives. Following on from this it is interesting that mesolithic burials are very rare in Scotland, with only a few human bones from late in the period known. Although there are many reasons for the absence of burials, from acid soils to traditions of research, one possibility is that the disposal of the dead at sea was important. Mesolithic burials in boats are known from Scandinavia, and it may be telling that the few bones that are known from the mesolithic in Scotland are found in shell middens on Oronsay. These are sites on the immediate coastline – a location that is sometimes perceived as being liminal, between land and water. Preservation biases are likely to be significant, as few inland locations have good conditions for faunal preservation, but given the factors outlined here an association in the later mesolithic between the sea, previous generations and death would not be surprising.

REVIEW

This chapter has outlined some of the processes being played out in the mesolithic period in Scotland. Discussions of North Atlantic circulation, or the speed with which tree species migrate may seem very distant from people's lives in the mesolithic, but the nature of the landscape in which people undertook their daily and seasonal rounds of tasks is vital to any attempt to understand how they came to know the world. Here I have stressed the dynamic, changing character of the mesolithic landscape, and it is clear that changes must have formed an important part of people's lives: as noted in the introduction, at times, models of the mesolithic have been rather generalised, or static. To my mind, the dynamism of the Scottish landscape demonstrates the need for more subtlety. This chapter also completes the setting of the scene for a more detailed discussion of people's lives in the mesolithic: this begins in the next chapter, with a close-grained focus on woodlands.

FURTHER READING

A range of further reading exists for landscape change in postglacial Scotland, but the reader should be warned that this is an area of interface between different disciplines and, consequently, an area where different academic languages meet. Specialised terminology is commonplace, and use of different dating systems (see chapter 1) a further source of confusion. That said, papers in recent review volumes (Ballantyne & Dawson 1997, Ballantyne 2004, Davidson & Carter 1997) offer good reviews, with detailed bibliographies, of physical landscape change: Ballantyne (2004) offers a very clear discussion of sea level change. Kevin Edwards and Richard Tipping are the leading palaeoenvironmental scholars in Scotland and their varied review papers (Edwards & Whittington 1997, Edwards 2004, Tipping 1994, 2004) give a very useful introduction. They sometimes disagree, and these discussions give an excellent flavour of debate at the interfaces of palaeoenvironmental reconstruction and archaeology. Tipping's 2004 paper includes details of sudden climatic changes, such as the 8200 event, with further references. David Smith and Caroline Wickham-Jones (2002) discuss the likely impact of the tsunami on mesolithic Scotland. Coles (1998) provides a stimulating, if sometimes technical, review of the changes in sea level across the North Sea plain. Kitchener et al. (2004) and McCormick & Buckland (1997) offer discussions of changing animal types. Finally Cramb (1998) offers an important reminder that environmental change is ongoing.

Ballantyne, C.K. and Dawson, A.G. 1997. 'Geomorphology and Landscape Change' in K.J. Edwards and I.B.M. Ralston (eds) *Scotland: Environment and Archaeology, 8000BC-AD 1000*, pp.23-44. (Edinburgh: John Wiley & Sons Ltd)

Ballantyne, C.K. 2004. 'After the Ice: Paraglacial and Postglacial evolution of the Physical Environment of Scotland, 20,000 to 5000 bp' in A. Saville (ed.) *Mesolithic Scotland and its Neighbours: the Early Holocene Prehistory of Scotland, its British and Irish context and some Northern European Perspectives*, pp.27-43. (Edinburgh: Society of Antiquaries of Scotland)

Coles, B.J. 1998. 'Doggerland: a speculative survey' in *Proceedings of the Prehistoric Society* 64: 45-81.

Cramb, A. 1998. *A Fragile Land: Scotland's Environment*. (Edinburgh: Polygon)

Davidson, D.A. and Carter, S.P. 1997. 'Soils and Their Evolution' in K.J. Edwards and I.B.M. Ralston (eds) *Scotland: Environment and Archaeology, 8000 BC-AD 1000*, pp.45-62. (Edinburgh: John Wiley & Sons Ltd)

Edwards, K.J. and Whittington, G. 1997. 'Vegetation Change' in K.J. Edwards and I.B.M. Ralston (eds) *Scotland: Environment and Archaeology, 8000 BC-AD 1000*, pp.63-82. (Edinburgh: John Wiley & Sons Ltd)

Edwards, K.J. 2004. 'Palaeoenvironments of the Late Upper Palaeolithic and Mesolithic Periods in Scotland and the North Sea Area: new work, new thoughts' in A. Saville (ed.) *Mesolithic Scotland and its Neighbours: the Early Holocene Prehistory of Scotland, its British and Irish context and some Northern European Perspectives*, pp.55-72. (Edinburgh: Society of Antiquaries of Scotland)

Kitchener, A.C., Bonsall, C. and Bartosiewicz, L. 2004. 'Missing Mammals from Mesolithic Middesn: a comparison of the Fossil and Archaeological Records for Scotland' in A. Saville (ed.) *Mesolithic Scotland and its Neighbours: the Early Holocene Prehistory of Scotland, its British and Irish context and some Northern European Perspectives*, pp.73-82. (Edinburgh: Society of Antiquaries of Scotland)

McCormick, F. and Buckland, P.C. 1997. 'Faunal Change: the vertebrate fauna' in K.J. Edwards and I.B.M. Ralston (eds) *Scotland: Environment and Archaeology, 8000 BC-AD 1000*, pp.83-108. (Edinburgh: John Wiley & Sons Ltd)

Smith, D.E. 2002. 'The Støregga Disaster' in *Current Archaeology* 179 (May 2002) pp.468-471

Tipping, R. 1994. 'The Form and Fate of Scotland's Woodlands' in *Proceedings of the Society of Antiquaries of Scotland* 124: 1-54

Tipping, R. 2004. 'Interpretative Issues Concerning the Driving Forces of Vegetation Change in the Early Holocene of The British Isles' in A. Saville (ed.) *Mesolithic Scotland and its Neighbours: the Early Holocene Prehistory of Scotland, its British and Irish context and some Northern European Perspectives*, pp.45-54. (Edinburgh: Society of Antiquaries of Scotland)

Wickham-Jones, C.R. 2002 'In Search of Squashed Mesolithic People' in *Current Archaeology* 179 (May 2002) pp.472-473

AN INTERJECTION

You keep mentioning coastal resources: whales, salmon and fishing trips. I hadn't really thought about hunter-gatherers doing very much fishing. I suppose it's in the name really – hunters and gatherers…

Exactly. There is a lot of debate about what hunter-gatherers should be called: hunter-gatherer, gatherer-hunter, hunter-gatherer-fisher, or fisher-hunter-gatherer – or any other combination of these words. We'll look at this in relation to food in chapter 4, but your point about fishing is well made. For some reason fishing has given anthropologists a hard time in terms of classifications of society and it is only relatively recently that it has seen a lot of critical attention. Broadly speaking there is a relationship between the amount people fish and the area in which they live: put crudely people seem to fish more the further north they live. Some writers have argued that there is a general relationship between the use of sea resources, especially abundant migratory fish, and the development of particular kinds of societies: those that live in one place for most of the year, and are characterised by inequality – like the coastal Northwest American groups I discussed earlier. Other writers, such as Gísli Pálsson, have suggested that we need to be careful about this relationship and have argued that this isn't due to environmental factors, but because of a complex of reasons to do with political relationships, especially in the near present.

But surely fishing requires lots of equipment and gear such as boats and nets, and if migratory fish are important then ownership of the fishing grounds must have been significant. Fishing must make a difference to relationships between people?

Right again. There is great debate about the ways in which the need for complex, specialist technology impacts on social relations – for example, making a boat or maintaining a static fish trap. Similarly concepts of ownership and the development of territoriality are often tied into these kinds of short-term abundant resources.

So can we assume that it was like this in Scotland?

Slow down! Fishing was certainly important to some communities in mesolithic Scotland but this doesn't mean that all of the other associated factors go alongside it. Certainly many writers have assumed that the resources of the sea were vital to mesolithic communities in Scotland, but our understanding of how the exploitation of these resources was organised is pretty poor, even in terms of the practicalities of landing catches, let alone the implications this has for social relations. We mustn't forget that hunter-gatherers in the modern world are hugely diverse, even after much colonial pressure, sometimes amounting to genocide. Hunter-gatherers in the past would have been much more diverse. We sometimes have a tendency to reach to anthropology and to general models to help make sense of our material – but always looking for the general means that we risk missing out on different ways of doing things. This leads to thinking about analogies, which are explored in the next chapter.

3

LIVING AMONG THE TREES

The previous discussions provide a broad context for thinking about mesolithic lives in Scotland: what the mesolithic was, and when it was. I have outlined the temporal scales at which one can come to know these people, and noted that the mesolithic likely contained much diversity. The last chapter reviewed the changing landscapes in which these people lived, from climate to sea level to woodlands. And yet the characteristics of mesolithic lives has remained absent. In the following chapters, I begin a more intimately focused discussion of the materiality of people's lives. This starts with the simple observation that the mesolithic experience of Scotland was that of a wooded landscape. A caveat, of course, is necessary. As touched upon in the last chapter and in the discussion that followed, for some, at least, of the mesolithic inhabitants of Scotland, the sea and other waterways provided a vital reference point. Rivers and a highly indented coastline would always have provided transport routes and resources (*28* and *29*). The seascapes and rivers of mesolithic Scotland have always witnessed academic attention, and this is explored in the next chapter. Here I stress woodlands, in part as a corrective to the dominance of water in most accounts of these people's lives, and in part in response to the genuine significance these features must have held.

INTRODUCTION

The modern visitor to a mesolithic site in Scotland is often underwhelmed. This is not surprising as there is frequently little to see. The view is simply of a ploughed field that contains a scatter of chipped stone tools; sometimes the site is a shoulder of hillside on which one can imagine a small settlement, but such images rely heavily on powerful modern cultural images of hunter-gatherers. Thus reconstruction drawings are filled with tee-pees or other tents: generic hunter-gatherers rather than anything specific. Shell middens provide one of the few constructions of the mesolithic that are visible

28 Seascape, from Mull. © *G. Warren*

today – but even these, at first glance, seem little more than heaps of shell. The visitor to a mesolithic site has little to help them in considering the realities of life lived among a collection of tents, or huts, the circles of activity around a campfire. In particular there is little chance to experience the constraints and opportunities architecture places on people, and the ways in which it structures people's experiences in historically specific ways: not for the mesolithic specialist the joys of walking the corridors of a village like Skara Brae or a tomb like Maes Howe.

An equally significant problem is the absence of trees from the modern landscape. The last chapter demonstrated that Scotland was covered by a variety of woodlands during the mesolithic period, and previous discussions noted that the mesolithic is often defined as a time period when gatherer-hunter communities adapted to dense woodlands. Yet today these trees are missing from the landscape, and, I will argue, are often strangely absent from most accounts of the period. This chapter considers the ways in which woodlands may have structured mesolithic experience. It first examines the character of these woodlands before turning attention to interactions with them. I outline one of the dominant metaphors for this relationship, the argument that mesolithic populations deliberately managed woodlands as part of their subsistence strategy, before considering alternative ways of conceptualising these relationships, and exploring some of the rhythms of living in woodland. These discussions also provide a useful context in which to consider the role of analogy in interpreting mesolithic lives.

THE CHARACTERISTICS OF WOODLAND

Many archaeologists have characterised the woodlands of mesolithic Scotland as dark and impenetrable: overgrown, foreboding places that were unattractive to settlement. Land routes were therefore considered to be impassable, and consequently mesolithic sites clung to the watery edges of the woods, on rivers, lakes or the coast. These

29 River Dee at Birkwood, Aberdeenshire. Rivers such as the Dee may have provided important axes of travel through Scotland. © G. Warren

dramatic images reflect real difficulties in understanding the natural woodlands of the early Holocene. They are also likely to be somewhat misleading. All of the woods we encounter in Britain today are the products of centuries of management, and literary representations colour modern images of virgin woodland: the forest of *Hansel and Gretel*; the Wild Wood of the *Wind in the Willows*; or the fearsome animated woodlands of Tolkien's Middle Earth. Perhaps importantly, these representations of woodland are the perspectives of a society dominated by farmers, and whose activity is opposed to the existence of woodland.

But natural woodlands are not like this. The original forests were dynamic communities in which disturbance was a vital part. Wind throw, lightning strikes, disease, soil changes, human activity, herbivore activity and sea level changes all contribute to the presence of gaps and variation within woodlands. The exact character of the primeval woodlands of north-western Europe is the subject of ongoing debate, with especial interest in the role of herbivores in creating and maintaining open spaces. Recent syntheses suggest that although herbivores were unlikely to have created substantial open spaces, they may have been significant in maintaining canopy openings created by other causes. Flood plains may have been important areas because of the frequency of natural clearings in these areas. In Scotland the after effects of glaciation included kettleholes and dumps of gravel. Mires were common, slowly infilling over the years. These were diverse woodlands, changing with altitude, relief, and, not least, over time. Scotland was also characterised by varied woodlands in different places (see chapter 3). The natural woodlands of Scotland were not impenetrable masses of deadwood and under-storey vegetation, although this may have been significant in some places, but were varied, with a range of habitats including open spaces.

Strangely enough, as well as characterising the mesolithic woodlands as dense and impenetrable, and whilst defining the mesolithic in terms of woodlands for many years, archaeologists have rather neglected the question of how mesolithic people actually lived in woodlands. Some scientists have produced remarkably detailed work on the

Left: 30 Birch tree. © *G. Warren*

Above: 31 Scots Pine. © *G. Warren*

characteristics of mesolithic woodlands, and there have been long debates about the role of human activity in influencing the development of woods. But in a general sense, archaeologists have seen woodlands in very broad-brush terms, as a background to mesolithic lives; a home for the animals hunted, a source of firewood, or as a general determinant of tactics of mobility and settlement. Richard Tipping has argued that we tend to see human activity as *opposed* to trees, rather than integrated with them. Mesolithic archaeologists have been much more reluctant to consider how peoples' daily lives were woven in and around trees: their structures, rhythms and textures (*30* and *31*). Possibly this subconsciously reflects the modern farmed landscape.

The shell middens of Cnoc Coig and Caisteal nan Gillean II on the island of Oronsay, for example, now stand in splendid isolation amidst grass, sand and rock and set back by isostatic uplift from the sea that they were once adjacent to. However the analysis of land-snail remains from both sites demonstrates that the middens were constructed in woodland. At Cnoc Coig the environment was a stabilising sand dune surface with ongoing woodland formation. At the time of occupation there was birch and hazel woodland in the immediate vicinity of the site (*32*): in fact, activity immediately around the midden may have stopped scrub woodland encroaching onto the site. At Caisteal nan Gillean II, analyses indicate denser woodland. Similar results have been obtained from the analysis of the contemporary midden at Morton, Fife, where heavily shaded dry woodland is indicated. These sites, and others throughout Britain, clearly indicate that in contrast to their modern appearance, at least some mesolithic settlements were woven in and around trees.

Looking ethnographically, hunter-gatherers from the Boreal north of America through to the Bushmen of Kalahari San also camp in and around trees. Notwithstanding their importance in terms of fuel and other resources or as symbolic reference points, trees form a vital part of the architecture of a campsite, used to provide privacy for toilet areas,

32 Modern birch woodland, Burn of Calleter, Angus.
© *G. Warren*

or for smaller groups of tents, used as shelter or shade, or a place to suspend food away from scavengers. It would not be appropriate to take any one example of these practices as an exact model for activity in mesolithic Scotland, but given that structures in Scotland were also constructed in woodlands it seems likely that trees played a similarly important role in structuring the use of space. But where are these trees in archaeological accounts? They are almost entirely absent.

Reconstruction drawings show these tendencies clearly – mesolithic structures are often presented in splendid isolation, with a fringe of woodland in the background. Of course, trees do not survive on most mesolithic sites, but just because something doesn't survive does not mean that we should neglect it when thinking about mesolithic experiences. This example is just one of the ways in which archaeologists have failed to consider the significance of woodlands in people's daily lives. These themes are returned to later in this chapter, but first it is important to consider the main argument proposed for mesolithic activity in woodlands – deliberate management in order to promote growth.

MANAGING WOODLANDS?

Since the 1960s analysts have noted that many pollen cores of mesolithic age were characterised by 'disturbance features', or are interruptions in what people supposed the natural sequence of vegetation in the area should be, often taking the form of a reduction in the proportion of trees. In the 1970s a number of archaeologists suggested that these disturbances were due to the behaviour of mesolithic people. Paul Mellars argued that small openings in the woods were very productive environments, producing much more herby vegetation and consequently attracting animals such as red deer. Drawing on a broad comparison with hunting and gathering communities in America, who were recorded as managing their woodlands by deliberate burning, Mellars proposed that mesolithic communities in Britain were similarly fire-managing woodlands in order to accrue benefits from clearings, most importantly by attracting red deer and easing their hunting. (In this context it should be noted that many of the early colonial descriptions of America focused heavily on the lush productive pastures and clearings in the forest, which were considered to be evidence of God's generosity in this wonderful new land. In fact the productivity of the forests, and their characteristic appearance, was greatly influenced by native American policies of land management – strategies that were not recognised by the colonists, who treated the New World as a vacant land for their possession.)

Arguments about the active mesolithic role in managing their woodlands rapidly caught on. Mesolithic man (and the gendered language is characteristic) was a 'fire raiser', involved in deliberately promoting the growth of hazel, elm and ivy, and collecting leaf fodder for animals. Mesolithic people were argued to have a very close relationship with red deer herds, with management that approached domestication. In recent years it has been argued, but not proven, that mesolithic people deliberately introduced red deer to Shetland in order to facilitate their colonisation of the island. Archaeologists studying the mesolithic in Europe argued for the possibility of effective domestication of wild boar. Although current understandings of the details are sketchy, some arguments have also been made that the initial mesolithic colonisation of Ireland, which took place by boat, involved transporting wild boar. It has been asserted that in Scotland mesolithic people practiced coppicing of woodlands in order to reap large harvests of hazel and wood. Extensive plant husbandry has been adduced, with the antler mattocks found in both east and west Scotland (*22*, *25* and *33*) seen as a vital part of the tool kit for these busy managers of natural resources. The extent of management was also seen as blurring the divide between the mesolithic hunter-gatherers of wild food and neolithic farmers of domesticated food. The popularity of these interpretations of mesolithic lives is striking, and it is arguably connected to a desire amongst archaeologists to identify mesolithic populations that were actively doing something.

Despite the popularity of these arguments, many problems exist with them in a Scottish context, and I am unconvinced that 'management' is the most helpful way of thinking about mesolithic woodland relations.

Firstly, the images of woodlands invoked in the models of management are at odds with the dynamic, disturbed environments described above, and seem to presuppose stable, dense forest, antithetical to mesolithic activity. It is also significant that many of Scotland's woodlands were very different in character to the woodlands of northern England – where there is the clearest evidence for the creation of clearings. The majority of woodland disturbance evidence comes from the south of Scotland, for example in Southern Uplands and over the border in the Cheviots. There is little evidence in the north-east and it is likely that the woodlands of this area, in which oak and elm never played a major role, did not witness the same types of activity. Recent studies in and around Oban, for example, have failed to find evidence of mesolithic woodland disturbance in an area of known settlement. Evidence from the examination of charcoal from a mesolithic structure at Nethermills, on the River Dee, also offers no indication of deliberate management of tree species – the material burnt on site would appear to be characteristic of a natural woodland structure. These varied strands of evidence suggest that management of woodlands may not be an appropriate way of considering the Scottish evidence. More specifically, in Scotland it is not clear that red deer played a dominant part in subsistence, and in fact there is evidence that at least some people were eating an exclusively marine diet in the last part of the mesolithic – not a context in which forest clearing is to be expected.

In terms of the 'management' argument, one should be suspicious of interpretations of mesolithic life that discuss cultural decisions to manipulate nature. Culture and nature are ambiguous terms, whose contemporary western meaning is far from universal. As discussed later in this chapter, many small-scale communities make little categorical distinction between culture and nature. It is likely to have been similar for mesolithic communities. Whenever we interpret mesolithic lives we must be careful not to import understandings from our modern lives into the past.

Management is also a rather ambiguous word. Managing a resource today can mean activity promoting its growth, or harvesting it in such a way that the resource is not impoverished – for example by limiting kill numbers, or only taking immature animals leaving a viable breeding population. Many archaeological accounts are not clear about what meaning is implied. Preconceptions of the characteristics of hunter-gatherer activity may also be significant here. Since the 1970s the increased political activism of indigenous peoples has included promotion of the image that hunter-gatherers are the original green community, who live in harmony with nature. In stark contrast with western degradations of the environment it is argued that foragers have maintained ecological equilibrium over the centuries. The green-fingered hunter-gatherer, repository of ecological knowledge, and embedded blissfully in nature is a powerful image, and arguably played an important role in the popularity of the management hypothesis. But it need not have been so. On a global scale hunter-gatherers have been associated with mass killings and even possibly extinctions, particularly when colonising new lands such as North America. In Scotland, evidence from Staosnaig, Colonsay, is of considerable interest. Here an abandoned house base was reused for depositing roasted hazelnuts at some time in the seventh millennium. Over 300,000 hazelnut shells were found, the product of around 5000 trees, which must have been harvested in a short time period, clear evidence of the very substantial use of plant resources by mesolithic communities. This 'nut fest' (to use Nyree Finlay's term) appears to be associated with a *decline* in the amount of hazel on the island. The evidence from Staosnaig either implies that mesolithic communities were not managing hazel, simply harvesting until the resource collapsed, or that if they were managing the resource they weren't very good at it. Of course other explanations are possible – population pressure for example – but Rob Sands has pointed out that the notion of people in the past being bad managers is rather uncomfortable; we like to think of people in the past as tuned into nature in a way that we aren't. And Staosnaig is not an isolated case. For example, evidence from Culverwell, Isle of Portland, on the south coast of England shows that mesolithic communities drastically overexploited local shellfish.

The final set of problems with models of mesolithic woodland management lies in the difficulty of interpreting pollen data. Whilst a clearing can be identified, it is much more difficult to establish whether the clearing is humanly or naturally established. Recent years have seen much debate about fire regimes in natural woodlands, and ways of differentiating between the evidence of campfires as opposed to burning strategies. The debate is far from over, but many analysts are much more cautious about identifying the hands of mesolithic communities behind every break in the woodland canopy. Even assuming that we can identify a deliberate clearance, the issue of why this clearing was created is complex. Returning to the North American comparison, it is clear that Native communities burnt the land for a wide variety of reasons including communication purposes and to deal with enemies. A more subtle approach may pay dividends. Tony Brown has argued that mesolithic and neolithic woodland lives must be understood in terms of opportunism. Accepting that natural clearings form a part of natural woodland dynamics he argues that we should be thinking about people colonising and possibly maintaining clearings of different types. Such strategies, which seem inherently plausible, would be very difficult to identify in the pollen record. Indeed, as noted above, it is likely that herbivores played an important role in maintaining clearances.

There are other possibilities. Maintaining a clearing by the riverside might have been a way of maintaining a relationship with the dead or the spirits who had lived there before (on occasion their white and gleaming stone tools would have been found when a pit was cut to throw rubbish in). Every year the campsite was cleared as the large groups gathered for the salmon run. Stopping the thick bracken from growing across the floodplain kept relations with the spirits in order, and kept the seasons turning, keeping the past and the present as one. Or perhaps burning a clearing came at the end of certain events, and was an act of closure for a location. Perhaps young trees were cleared so that an old oak with important carvings would remain easily visible. The oak might easily survive for 200-300 years, and the maintenance of this clearing over this time period might therefore create a 'disturbance episode' in the pollen record in the bog just down-slope. Of course, to an extent people are manipulating the environment, but in many senses this is an unintentional outcome of the actions that were being undertaken in the past. Archaeologists have tended to objectify these processes as human management or interference with nature rather than take seriously the possibility of alternative understandings of the world. It is to these alternatives that I now turn.

THE PICTURE FROM ETHNOGRAPHY AND THE DIFFICULTY WITH ANALOGY

Many modern small-scale cultivators and hunter-gatherers make little categorical distinction between culture and nature, human and non-human. Instead they understand the world in terms of relationships between different beings and forces – from animals and plants through weather systems, mountains and even down to rocks. These are described as 'relational epistemologies' (the term describes a way of understanding the world, and your place in it, as established through relationships rather than any *a priori* characteristics) or sometimes, more broadly, as a form of 'animism'. Mesolithic people also came to understand the world in terms of their relationships to various aspects of it. But how might mesolithic people have understood these relationships?

A lot of work has been done on the how modern (rain) forest dwelling foragers understand the world. The anthropologist Nurit Bird-David has argued that many forest dwelling hunter-gatherers see the forest as nurturing them. The Mbuti of Zaire and the Nyaka of Tamil Nadu, for example, consider themselves to be children, and the forest as parent. Here the forest spirits are generally seen as benevolent and supportive. However, some hunter-gatherers, such as the Koyukon of Alaska, perceive the spirits to be hostile, and attempt to propitiate them by closely adhering to traditional ways of behaviour. Some cultivators also understand the world through relational epistemologies. The Bette and the Nulle Kurumba of southern India, for example, believe that they have reciprocal relationships with ancestral spirits and the environment. Here they must obtain favour through certain behaviour. The distinction is highlighted most clearly by the fact that whilst Nyaka (forest hunter-gatherers) offer honey to the forest spirits *after* collection as a gift of thanks, cultivators make offerings at the *beginning* of harvest and sowing in order to ensure the success of their actions.

These ways of understanding hunter-gatherer perception of the environment offer a level of resolution and detail that cannot be obtained through archaeological analysis. It would be very tempting to choose one of these examples and say 'it was like *that*'. This kind of argument is known as an analogy. It takes two different situations, separated by both space and time, and saying that because they are similar in some ways (all hunter-gatherers, or all living in forests) they are actually similar in other ways (in this instance, the ways in which they understand the environment). Analogies are an important, but controversial, part of archaeological interpretation; two have featured strongly in this chapter. The discussion of the role of trees in structuring space drew parallels with other hunter-gatherer sites, and the review of Paul Mellars' arguments about management noted his American comparisons.

Understanding the use of analogies is a vital part of learning to think archaeologically; and in general archaeologists are suspicious of detailed, specific analogies. The discussion of the ways in which woodlands structured the use of settlement areas earlier in this chapter argued that whilst archaeologists couldn't say that trees were used to shelter a toilet, or hang meat from, they could say that trees were probably used to structure space. I should possibly have been more cautious and explicit, and stated that the analogy showed that some people who lived in environments with trees used trees as part of the structure of their campsite. Therefore it seems possible that mesolithic communities in a wooded country like Scotland also made use of trees to structure space. But this is a long-winded way of saying something. I'm sorry to labour this point, but it is important – analogies are vital to making sense of things, both in the present day and in archaeology: we are always comparing things we don't know with things that we do.

In the example of the relationships with the spirits above, it is not clear what detailed analogy would fit best. The forest hunter-gatherers seem broadly analogous to woodland hunter-gatherers at one level. Perhaps then, and following Bird-David, one might speak of the woodlands of Scotland as being perceived as 'parent' to hunter-gatherers? No. The communities Bird-David discusses are rain forest hunter-gatherers, living in a very different environment, and with different subsistence strategies. What of the Koyukon? Again, these are different environments. The cultivators of southern India might seem very different – they are after all not hunter-gatherers. But care is needed here. Why should all hunter-gatherers be alike? And why should they be different to farmers? In fact *none* of the details of the relationships described above are appropriate. All I can say is that the broad relational epistemology, rather than a split between nature and culture, is characteristic of many small-scale communities today, including hunter-gatherers and cultivators in a range of environments (in fact in this context, it is modern Western ideas that look like the odd one out). Given this broad pattern it is likely that hunter-gatherers in Scotland in the past held broadly similar relational epistemologies, and that much of their activity in the landscape was seen to involve interactions with animate spirits or ancestors. The analogy alone cannot tell us how this relationship was understood, but we might possibly find other evidence to help make sense of it.

LIVING IN WOODLANDS

We begin to move closer to an understanding of how mesolithic lives may have been interwoven with the woodlands that surrounded them. Far from clinging to the edges of an impenetrable woodland, mesolithic people were wood-dwellers. As such their lives were entangled with the rhythms and other inhabitants of those woods. The final section of this chapter examines some of these interplays.

The mesolithic experience of woodlands was marked by varied rhythms. At the largest of scales the mesolithic period saw the migration of trees, over a period of thousands of years. At smaller scales, every day was divided into night and day, and the woodlands were different in both: nocturnal animals, such as wolves, may have made the night woodlands a more difficult prospect than that of the day. In this context the fact that many parts of Scotland are marked by a great seasonality of daylight is also striking. Mesolithic populations of the Orkney Isles, if they remained on the islands during winter, would have had little more than six hours of daylight a day. I am grateful to Caroline Wickham-Jones for the reminder that in these areas the light of the moon and stars and the Aurora Borealis may have been central to people's routines. The timescales of human lives were also entwined with the trees: younger children could climb higher into the canopy to poach eggs from nests located on thinner boughs.

Living in a predominantly deciduous environment would have had many impacts on the experience of time and seasonality (33). One characteristic of woodlands, for example, is the vernal period, a short period of time in early spring when ground shrubs and grasses flourish before leaf cover blocks out their sources of light – the most famous example would be the dominance of bluebells in contemporary woodlands. In contrast, late spring and early summer was a time of abundant green growth; visibility was low and quiet movement

33 Deciduous woodlands, Tweed Valley. © G. Warren

more difficult. Late summer may have been noted as a time when berries and other fruits were abundant. The varied tastes associated with differing times of the year would have been closely caught up in rhythms of growth and harvest and would have provided one of the fundamental ways of structuring the personal and communal experience of time. For example the Achuar, small-scale horticulturists of the Upper Amazon, call the period from November to April the 'time of the wild fruits', whilst March is the 'time of the fat of the woolly monkey' and September to January is the ' time of the fish'. In a similar fashion the pygmies of the Ituri forest celebrate the honey season.

Vision and mobility in deciduous woodlands would also be closely linked to the seasons. The winter was characterised by dead wood and little vegetation, mobility was at its height and movement was relatively easy, if muddy or snowy. Breath frosted in the air. Animals must have been easier to track in these conditions. Rivers, presumably important as communication routes, would also have been seasonal. They would have run in spate in spring for example, but lower in autumn. This seasonal transformation from trickle to torrent had effects upon mobility both up and down river and across it. Again, the details escape analysis, but the structuring principle of the changing woodlands must have been vital.

Discussing woodland and mobility requires a consideration of paths (*colour plate 9*). Some routes through the trees were long established – the track to the riverside from the tents themselves, or the route onto the floodplain for the large gatherings of the community. Other routes were trod once and once only. In a similar way old paths from a previous year's visit towards good hunting grounds may still have been viable and could be retrodden. Possibly some spring and summer growth needed to be cut back in order to maintain important routes. Some people may have outlasted particular paths, whereas some paths had always been there. Treading the same paths as a now deceased parent, or an elder sibling now married, may have been an important part of the biography of particular individuals. Paths had differing durations and the scar of erosion created by the routines of labour may, in turn, have shaped the activity of those following. Particular routes through the trees created certain views and vistas – in a very subtle way structuring a community's experience of the local world. Learning traditional paths, their names and the names of features of the landscape visible from these routes were a vital aspect of socialisation.

There would also have been relationships with time and space established by moving through a wooded environment marked, in places, by human agency: the scar of a path, debris from a fire or flint scatter, or in places a small clearing. Mesolithic people were certainly adept interpreters of the forest they grew up within. For example, for the Meratus of South Kalimantan, Indonesia:

> The landscape is known as a patchwork not only of (these) vegetational types but also of specific places. Large, emergent trees often have individual names – not just species names – which can be used to identify particular groves and hill sides. Through foraging, travelling, and memories of old fields regrown into forest, central-mountain Meratus become familiar with a number of forest sites. As the sites themselves take on overlapping and varied social connotations, each user gains a loose sense of connection with other users past and present. Social identities in the mountains are not forged in 'domesticated' villages; they take on the complexity of associations with the forest landscape as a fabric of diverse social and natural resources.
>
> Lowenthal-Tsing, A. 1993. *In the Realm of the Diamond Queen: Marginality in an Out-of-the-Way Place* p.62. (Princeton)

It is likely to have been similar for mesolithic inhabitants of Scotland. Old campsites could be recognised, or regrowth in clearings highlighted. Carvings on trees could outlast individuals, persisting over the centuries in some instances, warping and twisting as the tree grew, establishing links between different generations and the past.

An important characteristic of mesolithic woodlands is that they were occupied by much more than just people and trees. Today wild animals are so rare, especially in woodland, that it is unusual to spot them. In the past, however, the woodlands of Scotland were shared with, to name but some of the larger animals, red deer, roe deer, elk, aurochs (wild cattle), wild boar, bear and wolf. Whilst many were prey some were dangerous adversaries if cornered, or powerful enough to pose a threat to a campsite. It is perhaps not too fanciful to image a small party of hunters, slow to butcher their prey, casting eyes over their shoulders at the gathering pack of scavenging wolves.

Of course, as noted above, many animals would have been perceived within a relational epistemology. Animals and humans may have been considered in some ways as equals and hunting as an intimate and delicate way of managing this relationship, rather than simply as a source of food. For many northern hunter–gatherers, animals and humans are bound in relationships of trust and respect and are not considered separate: indeed some individuals have the ability to take on the forms of either animals or humans at different times. Animals may, in some ways have been understood as totems, or at the very least provided powerful metaphors by which human experiences were understood. For many hunting and gathering groups bears are an important symbolic reference point, not least because of their broadly anthropogenic appearance. Wolves are social animals living in groups, which may have been seen as analogous to human social organisation. Christopher Tilley has argued that mesolithic communities in Scandinavia saw themselves as analogous to red deer populations. The animals of Scottish woodlands and coasts were a vital part of the ways in which people came to terms with the world around them. Discussion in the following chapters builds upon these points.

REVIEW

At the outset of this chapter I stated that the woodlands of mesolithic Scotland had been dealt with rather strangely by archaeologists. On the one hand they were considered the dark antithesis of human action, whilst on the other described as defining that action. Vast time and energy has been expended on reconstructing the history of woodlands, but there has been little critical thought about how people may have lived *in* woodlands – and most of the time it is as if archaeologists have tacitly assumed that people somehow lived in front of them. There are genuine problems here, for the trees are lost. Archaeologists can never reconstruct the alder carr surrounding the river or sit under the old oak that sheltered part of the clearing. But we should not forget the influence of the trees, both individually and as a woodland community. Many mesolithic communities were woodland dwellers (I say many, because some may have lived primarily on and by the sea) and the woodlands were not just a stage backdrop to their action, but *the* vital context in which biographies were extended. I also stated that mesolithic lives had refused resolution to the discussions in this book so far. I hope that this chapter has begun to effect the change in focus needed to identify mesolithic lives – examining, in a more fine-grained fashion, the interactions between people and their social environments. Mesolithic identity was forged in woods that were practical and symbolic resources and one of the ever-presents of life. These woodlands, in turn, demand critical thought as we try and interpret those lives.

FURTHER READING AND REFERENCES

The character of woodlands, and the relationships between hunter-gatherers and the forests they inhabited has been the focus of increasing analytical attention. Peterken and Vera have both made substantial contributions to debate on the structure of natural woodlands in northwestern Europe, and have helped challenge understandings of these spaces. Tipping (1994) and the papers from Edwards and Ralston's edited volume discussed in chapter 2 give more Scottish detail. Aspects of the management debate can be seen in Paul Mellar's classic 1976 article. Marek Zvelebil develops many of these arguments in a recent model of hunter-gatherers actively promoting the growth of many wild resources (1994). Shepard Krech III offers a critical appraisal of the myth of hunter-gatherers as original environmentalists (1999) and Mithen et al. (2001) and Mannion (2002) offer British examples of resource depletion. Nurit Bird-David's papers (1990, 1999) are classic anthropological pieces.

Bird-David, N.H. 1990. 'The giving environment: another perspective on the economic system of gatherer-hunters'. *Current Anthropology* 31: 189-196

Bird-David, N.H. 1999. '"Animism" Revisited: personhood environment and relational epistemology'. *Current Anthropology* S40: 67-91

Krech, S. 1999. *The Ecological Indian: myth and history.* (Norton)

Mannino, M.A. and Thomas, K.D. 2002. 'Depletion of a Resource? The impact of prehistoric foraging on intertidal mollusc communities and its significance for human settlement, mobility and dispersal' in *World Archaeology* 33(3) pp.452-474

Mellars, P.A. 1976. 'Fire Ecology, Animal Populations and Man: a study of some ecological relationships in prehistory' in *Proceedings of the Prehistoric Society* 42: 15-45

Mithen, S., Finlay, N., Carter, S. and Ashmore, P. 2001. 'Plant Use in the Mesolithic: evidence from Staosnaig, Isle of Colonsay, Scotland' in *Journal of Archaeological Science* 28: pp.223-234

Peterken, G.F. 1996. *Natural Woodland: ecology and conservation in Northern Temperate Regions.* (Cambridge: Cambridge University Press)

Tipping, R. 1994. 'The Form and Fate of Scotland's Woodlands' in *Proceedings of the Prehistoric Society* 124: 1-54

Vera, F. 2000. *Grazing Ecology and Forest History.* (Cabi)

Zvelebil, M. 1994. 'Plant Use in the Mesolithic and its Role in the Transition to Farming' in *Proceedings of the Prehistoric Society* 60: 35-74

34 Hammerstone (Rink Farm) and Anvil (Manor Bridge). Scale bar at 1cm intervals. © *G. Warren*

AN INTERJECTION

This is all interesting enough. But aren't we losing track of some of the archaeological materials? You're using lots of interesting analogies, but I expected to hear more about the kinds of objects you find on sites, and how you use these to understand the kinds of things people did.

Forgive me. We're getting there. As I stated at the outset, I'm trying to narrow the focus, all the time giving the kinds of contexts I think are important to making sense of the data that we do actually have. In fact, if you look closely, there's quite a lot of evidence in everything so far.

Maybe so. I just thought that one of the things I'd be finding out about in this book would be some of the basics: making stone tools, what they were used for and so on. You mentioned this a bit at the start, and I think I've got some of the key terms — blades, cores and microliths — but I can't see how to relate this to all this talk of metaphors and relational epistemologies. I'm still not sure about how people make stone tools, let alone use them to understand their world in complex symbolic ways!

I suppose the key point would be that even in the mesolithic people learnt the symbolic aspects of stone tool working as they learnt the practical — it's not as if the symbolic beliefs were plastered onto practical competencies: the two arose together, in the context of getting on with daily life. We'll be looking at this in detail in chapter 5 in particular, and I hope that things will become clearer then. But maybe a few more details on stone tools will help set the scene.

The basics of stone crafting in the mesolithic of Britain are quite straightforward. Stone working is based on the interaction between the skills of the craftsperson and the fracture properties of particular kinds of rocks. The best kinds of rocks are fine grained and homogenous — these tend to be silica materials. Flint is one of the best types, although lots of other rocks are also quite good: chert, chalcedony, mudstones, even things like quartz. Good sources of flint are rare in Scotland, so people used a wide range of raw materials. This is actually quite useful to us as archaeologists, as we can compare the use of different materials, and think about where people had to go to get particular resources (*colour plate 10*).

Stone working mainly focused on the production of blades, those elongated parallel-sided stone tools that I discussed briefly in chapter 1 (see *8, 9* and *11*). Making a blade involved the careful preparation of a pebble or nodule into a core, which had a flat area with just the right edge angle from which to make removals. Using a hammer (*34*), and possibly a punch, a stone worker would strike a blow at the very edge of the flat area on the core (the platform): the force from this blow would remove a piece from the core. Generically, these removals are called flakes; blades are a sub set of these. In Scotland these blades are generally small — often less than 5cm in maximum length. Modifying the edges of blades and flakes makes other tools, such as scrapers. Microliths are made by modifying blades using a combination of snapping and edge adjustment.

4

THE STUFF OF LIFE

This chapter considers the ways in which the hunter-gatherers of the mesolithic in Scotland obtained some of the necessary materials for life, from foodstuffs through medicine to the raw materials for the manufacture of items of material culture. This chapter therefore looks at the stuff of life for mesolithic communities, and explores the ways in which the procurement of resources provides a key into qualities of mesolithic lives in Scotland. These themes, for example the ways in which skills and materiality coalesce in particular rhythms of labour, are returned to throughout the following chapters. Here I begin by thinking about the difficulties, particularly the assumptions that have surrounded attempts to understand these processes. I then sketch the beginnings of alternative narratives.

WHAT IS IT FOR?

Archaeologists have often argued that one of the easiest aspects of ancient societies to understand is their technology and economy – note for example the emphasis on mesolithic people as hunter-gatherers. Working with material culture and ecological remains archaeologists supposed that technology and economy were key to interpretations of the past. Building from this only later, and with difficulty, could archaeologists think about social relations, ideology and the like. There are several interesting assumptions embedded in this way of thinking. Firstly, technology and the economy are considered to be separate from social relations, ideology or symbolism; a particularly modern way of thinking about the world. Secondly, these kind of technological and economic issues – the dull compulsion of daily life – are considered interpretable through fairly simple, often common sense, assumptions. Thus the first questions about an artefact are often about its function: what was it used for? Very often the answers to this tend to be very practical in nature. These assumptions about use can be quite problematic.

  Take, for example, these perforated pebbles found in the Tweed Valley in surface scatters associated with mesolithic artefacts (35). Their date is not clear, but they seem most likely to be mesolithic. They are found with other mesolithic artefacts in Scotland,

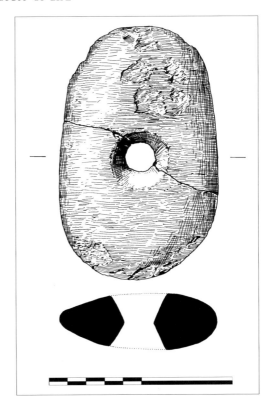

35 Perforated stone tool from 'Tweedside'.
Redrawn from Lacaille 1954. Reproduced at
1:2. © G. Warren

and are paralleled by mesolithic perforated stone artefacts in Scandinavia and in southern England. Numerous interpretations are possible for these simple objects, they may for example be mace heads, hammer heads or the weights from digging sticks. All of these explanations are plausible – but it is also interesting that they are all practical. In contrast, recent work in the Papua New Guinea highlands has shown that identical artefacts are sacred power stones *(bumkil)*, some of which are slipped over roof posts in order to protect the house from spirits. Which interpretation seems more likely for the archaeological examples? We would probably be more likely to assume the practical one. But why should we assume this? (Of course, for the Yali the business of keeping their roof spiritually protected is an eminently practical one.) As argued in the last chapter, using ethnographic analogies for the mesolithic in Scotland is problematic, but this example highlights well that assumptions about practical uses may be misplaced.

In some instances it is not necessary to make such bold assumptions about the uses of objects. Functional analyses of stone tools, for example, allow reconstructions – in some detail – of what artefacts were used for. The most common of these processes is known as 'microwear'. This involves manufacturing experimental tools and using them on a range of materials. The microscopic patterns of damage to the working edge caused to the tools through different uses are then recorded with characteristic patterns of fracture and polish identified. Archaeological examples of similar tools are studied, and the patterns of damage compared to the experimentally produced material.

The technique can identify the broad kinds of materials worked by tools, and the main type of use. Interestingly, the results from microwear show great variation between sites – even between those using the same tools. Take for example the sites of Gleann Mor and Bolsay Farm, both on Islay. Both sites include a particular type of microlith, called a scalene triangle. Yet on the two sites the scalene triangles are made differently, and used for slightly different things. Scalene triangles at Bolsay Farm often have transverse wear patterns associated with shaving of different materials whilst those at Gleann Mor have longitudinal wear associated with cutting. There are also differences in the materials worked: at Bolsay Farm these are much harder than at Gleann Mor. This implies that, not only is it difficult to assume that things must have a practical use, but that it is difficult to assume that they have the same use in different places. This in turn raises a series of questions about whether objects only had one use, or were used for a range of things.

Problems persist when considering the location of sites. Many archaeologists have assumed, despite lots of ethnographic evidence to the contrary, that hunter–gatherer sites are located simply because of proximity to food sources. Detailed models showing the relationship between sites and their local environments have been produced, all based on the simple assumption that people living on a site will exploit all of the resources in its immediate locality. This seems, again, like a common sense and straightforward enough assumption. But it masks a number of problems. Take, for instance, the distribution of sites along the major rivers of eastern Scotland. On the River Tweed many mesolithic sites sit on outcrops above the river, or large terraces near pools – often in locations that, today, are famous for their salmon fishing. Manor Bridge, near Peebles, for example, is a good spot for autumn fishing (*colour plate 3*), whilst Rink Farm, at the junction of the Tweed and Ettrick is a prime spring fishing location, as salmon wait for the spring melt (*36*). On the Dee the mesolithic structure at Nethermills, downstream of Banchorry, has been interpreted as a fishing settlement (*37*). Often, in these examples, the location of the sites is seen to give a simple indication of their economic role: they are by good salmon spots, salmon are a predictable and abundant resource in the modern landscape, therefore they must be for salmon fishing. Perhaps. But, as discussed above, there is actually very little evidence for salmon fishing at these sites and instabilities in the salmon resource in the mesolithic may have been an important reason for people to avoid relying heavily on it. It is possible that the interest in salmon has overshadowed alternative reasons for occupying these sites. For example at both Manor Bridge and the Dookits, also near Peebles, mesolithic activity has taken place on rocky outcrops immediately adjacent to the Tweed (*colour plates 3 and 11*). Looking ethnographically, there is a range of evidence to suggest that hunter–gatherer sites may be located near significant spiritual landmarks, for example important rock outcrops. Vicky Cummings has argued that some mesolithic sites in South Wales are located with respect to dramatically coloured cliffs: at Cwm Bach, for example, a flint scatter is found in the vicinity of distinct black, grey and orange cliffs and purple pebbles, and similar patterns are observed at Porth Y Rhaw and Swanlake. Furthermore, and as discussed in more detail in chapter 6, rivers themselves may have held important symbolic associations to hunting and gathering communities.

36 View to Rink Farm (main area of site indicated by arrow), Scottish Borders. Ettrick Water flows from left, Tweed from middle. Note: this photograph shows the old bridge, the modern bridge runs immediately downstream. *After Mason 1931*

It is therefore possible that the location of mesolithic sites on rocky outcrops by the Tweed is not simply because of the distribution of food sources but arises in part from understandings of the spiritual or mythological nature of the landscape. Of course, human nature is rather complex, and the search for a single reason for a given activity is likely to be too reductionist: decisions about resources were always embedded in other understandings.

More work is needed to clarify this issue, but perhaps enough has been said to question the simple assumption that location in the modern landscape bears a straightforward relationship to the exploitation of resources in the mesolithic. In any case, it is important to ask what kinds of narratives are created for the mesolithic by these assumptions about people in the past being driven solely by the need to procure resources. I would argue strongly that they are limiting assumptions, that create an impoverished understanding of mesolithic lives. They are also not necessary assumptions; it is possible to approach the material in different ways.

THINKING ABOUT FOOD

Another powerful suite of assumptions operate when considering diet. Looking globally human diets are exceptionally varied, and often surrounded by strong cultural prejudices. Many examples could be offered of meals that modern westerners consider unpalatable but are eaten by many other cultures: insects are guaranteed to turn the stomach. Even within the modern west certain foods carry powerful associations – the fear of being forced to eat snails and frogs legs used to colour my childhood visits to France. This

37 View towards site of Nethermills, above River Dee, Aberdeenshire. © *G. Warren*

highlights the ways in which eating or not eating particular types of food is caught up in group identity, perhaps most clearly in food taboos – that Hindus will not eat beef, nor vegans any animal products for example. The extent of proscriptions surrounding food is also clear in the production of Halal meat – animals killed in the appropriate ways according to Islamic belief. In a similar fashion, for many contemporary hunter-gatherers the process of consuming animal food is associated with the need to treat the remains of the animal in the correct manner – by depositing parts of the body with care and respect, thus ensuring that the spirit of the animal returns to the spirit master. As Richard Chatterton has recently demonstrated, examples of the deliberate deposition of animal carcases can be identified in the mesolithic of Britain.

Another possible example of complex cultural attitudes to food in early prehistory can be seen in one of the most striking features of the end of the mesolithic period in western Scotland, at around 4000-3800 BC, when analysis of human bone chemistry data seems to suggest a sudden and dramatic shift away from the consumption of marine proteins to a reliance on terrestrial animals protein. The analytical technique is isotope analysis of human bone. This technique works on the principle that the foods we consume contribute directly to the structure of our body: we literally are what we eat. All foodstuffs have a signature formed of different stable isotopes, and these signatures are preserved, although with some modification, as they pass through the food chain. Measuring stable isotopes of bone therefore allows an assessment of the food used in building that bone. Attention has focused upon carbon and nitrogen isotopes ($\delta^{13}C$ and $\delta^{15}N$). These isotopes allow an assessment of the contribution of varied forms of protein to an individual's diet. In particular, it is possible to distinguish between proteins derived from terrestrial and marine animals and to gain a sense of the place of the animal on the food chain. From this, reasonable estimates can be made about the kinds of things people must have eaten. This is a very powerful technique, and has made significant contributions to understandings of mesolithic life although the number of individuals examined is very small, and aspects of the analysis are controversial. Strikingly, and in keeping with data from across Europe, the evidence implies that at the end of the mesolithic communities were often heavily reliant on marine protein, but appear to have 'turned their back' on the resources of the sea with the arrival of domesticated animals and grain. Maritime resources were still plentiful in the region, and people were still travelling by boat – in fact there is actually increased evidence for mobility around the Irish Sea. These arguments are controversial, but it has been proposed that the decision not to eat marine resources by the first farmers in the region might actually be an example of a food taboo of some kind, or of a conscious decision to distance themselves from hunter-gatherer food.

It is also important to note that food fashions change. It is interesting that modern luxury foods, such as oysters, smoked salmon and wild mushrooms, were all once considered peasant food. A Scottish mesolithic meal may have included oysters, smoked salmon, wild venison with wild garlic and mushrooms followed by freshly collected berries. In fact there are many shell middens on the east coast of Scotland composed almost entirely of oyster shells – at Nether Kinneil, Polmont, Inveravon and Grangemouth on the Forth for example. Although the dates of these middens are controversial, at least some of the activity is likely to have been mesolithic. Oysters themselves offer a very good example of differing attitudes to food: some consider them a delicacy; others think that they are disgusting. Of course, you learn how to like oysters, by being placed in particular social contexts. And oysters therefore demonstrate how 'taste' is caught up in class and social identity. This is important, because embedded attitudes about food have been very powerful in maintaining an image of impoverished mesolithic communities.

Prejudices about food can be seen operating very clearly in discussions of mesolithic shell middens, for example. Many mesolithic shell middens contain large amounts of limpet (*38*); the Oronsay middens, for example, are dominated by limpets. Further north, on the mainland opposite Skye a shell midden at Sand is dominated by limpet with large quantities of dogwhelk, periwinkle and mussel (see *6*). Many of these species, but particularly limpet, are generally considered poor food by modern palates – their peculiar rubbery texture considered most unappealing. Limpets are often described as starvation food, reflecting how they were used historically in parts of Scotland. This has provoked much debate about the status of the middens themselves – are the accumulations of shell the results of meals, or are they derived from baiting lines for fish, for which there are many historical examples?

These arguments are interesting, but also revealing. Again mesolithic activity is seen, fairly straightforwardly, in economic terms. In any case, middens are more varied than this in composition: to the east, at Morton, cockles dominate, with mussel and crab claws also present. Also in the east, at Muirtown, Inverness and, as noted above, in the estuary of the Forth, middens are composed almost exclusively of oyster shell. The composition of middens reflects the availability of species in the environment surrounding the site. Nevertheless, in many interpretations, middens, with what we today perceive as unpleasant foods, are seen to be a by-product of economic need, whichever the system of mobility: either the by-product of fishing, or of times of hardship, even of the long-term hardship of a particular way of life.

Perhaps, however, there is more to shell middens than this: again, it is necessary to explore a multitude of possible associations and meanings. Recent approaches to middens in northern Europe have argued that they may have played a role in feasting, and that temporary abundances of food – such as limpets – may have enabled larger groups of people to come together for short periods of time. Although these arguments are not appropriate for all middens, they help reconsider the processes by which middens were formed. Middens vary, from small deposits of material through to substantial mounds, and it is important to stress that the accumulation of middens is not an accidental by-product of eating shellfish or baiting lines. Some middens were accumulations of debris deliberately built up over long time-periods, with later activity deliberately located on top of a large, presumably uncomfortable and smelly, pile of shells. This clear choice probably served as a way of associating your actions with those of the generations before. At times, these associations were very explicit, at other times hardly thought of, but the material mass of the midden provided a powerful mnemonic (an aid to memory). In this regard it is very interesting that the Oronsay middens include small fragments of human bones, and may have played a role in funerary rites. Other middens were smaller, and shorter lived.

Not simply to do with starvation food, or economics, recent analyses of middens addresses a wider series of concerns. We will discuss middens in more detail later on; at this stage it is important to note that assumptions that gathering and disposing of food are simply practical activities, devoid of any wider sets of meanings, are difficult to sustain. This is also true of procuring raw materials for tool manufacture. Activities that are dismissed as to do with 'technology' are clearly very socially specific, involving particular learnt structures of behaviour: as such this kind of evidence is very informative about the conditions within which people came to understand their world.

HUNTER–GATHERER OR GATHERER–HUNTER?

Very powerful assumptions have surrounded the potential roles of hunting, gathering and fishing to the diet of mesolithic communities. For many years archaeologists had assumed that hunting was the dominant way in which 'hunter-gatherers' obtained their sustenance. Hunting of large game was closely associated with male activity, and dominant models stressed the role of 'Man the Hunter' in the process of human evolution. Women's role in this model of how 'hunter-gatherers' worked was often little more than to raise children, provide some green and leafy accompaniment to the meat brought home by their partners, and swoon in appreciation of the food provided for them. This heavily gendered image is carried over in many reconstruction drawings of the period. Unsurprisingly, this model, with its clear origins in idealisations of contemporary gender divisions, was soon criticised and a variety of work was undertaken that showed that in

38 Limpets. © *G. Warren*

many instances it was 'Woman the Gatherer' who provided most of the food, and that men, when they did eventually actually manage to kill something, were simply providing dietary variation. Strikingly, even in some of the toughest environments – such as the Kalahari desert – the role of plant foods is still greater than that of meat. Still later, scholars began stressing the importance of fish, and many models that connected fishing with certain kinds of hunting and gathering societies were constructed, highlighting, for example, that fishing communities tended to be sedentary rather than mobile, and are often hierarchical: what are sometimes called 'complex hunter-gatherers'. We have touched upon this argument in discussion already and will return to it later.

In this regard it is important to stress differences in attitudes to different kinds of food. Just as many people today consider meat central to their diet many hunter-gatherers place significance on hunted meat of larger animals, even when the main calorific basis of subsistence is gathered foodstuffs. In this scenario male activity is seen as culturally significant, not least because large animals were often shared in prescribed ways amongst the community, whereas women's roles in gathering and hunting small animals is neglected.

The dominant popular image of the British mesolithic is probably that of men hunting red deer. The excavation at Star Carr, North Yorkshire, from 1949-1951 was one of the projects that defined the mesolithic period. The site has a large assemblage of worked stone, bone and antler as well as extensive animal remains, which enabled unusually detailed reconstructions of the animals present on site. One of the most dramatic finds were red deer antler frontlets that had been slightly modified to facilitate their use as some kind of headpiece. Interpretations ranged from shamanic headdresses to disguises used to enable the hunter to move closer to his prey before using his bow and arrow – the second key symbol of the period. The microlith is the mesolithic find *par excellence*, and for many years was interpreted as part of a projectile point (*39*). Red deer, microliths, hunting and the mesolithic therefore all went together on the most influential British site. Models derived from this site proposed that the seasonal movements of people mimicked those of the red deer they hunted, and later arguments claimed that red deer may have been semi-domesticated, or that management of clearings was to encourage aggregations of red deer. The story of the mesolithic was an androcentric tale of hunting large game.

Today archaeologists are much more critical of such narratives. Nyree Finlay has robustly critiqued the equation of mesolithic with large game hunting, arguing that this created a mesolithic dominated by male activity, characterised by 'boys and arrows' narratives. Reinterpretations of Star Carr have shown that red deer was not even the dominant foodstuff on site but that aurochs (wild cattle) provided most of the meat. Microliths have been demonstrated to have been used for many different purposes, not simply as projectiles. Scholars have stressed the range of biases that lead us to emphasise the dominance of large game – ranging from the cultural emphasis placed on meat today to the fact that big bones from large mammals are more likely to be preserved and discovered on archaeological sites than small bones are, thus meaning that evidence for large game is easier to find.

In fact, on *a priori* grounds it is very difficult to assume anything beyond very broad generalisations about the hunter-gatherer economy in Scotland. Writers have argued that most communities reliant on plants live in warmer environments than Scotland, and that the seasonality at such a northerly latitude is too extreme to allow plants to provide a year-round basis for the diet. Even given changes in the climate – see chapter 3 – this seems likely. We might expect significant seasonal variation in the diet of mesolithic communities, possibly ameliorated by storage of some foodstuffs for the cold winter months. We might also expect variation over time, although the data presently refuses resolution.

MAKING PATTERNS

These examples about obtaining food highlight that it is very difficult to assume anything about the character of procurement of resources. Assumptions, be it regarding an economic sphere of activity, or about the particular kind of resource desired, reveal a great deal about archaeological preconceptions and preoccupations – but they may obscure the details of mesolithic lives. Many of the assumptions about economics and diet made by archaeologists studying the hunter-gatherer period can be seen as an attempt to reconstruct the economic system used by those communities. Despite ethnographic evidence to the contrary, many archaeologists still suppose that they will eventually be able identify stable patterns of movement and exploitation. Thus, they hope that they will be able to track how these communities lived at different times of the year and create models of how subsistence was organised across the landscape as a whole. The dominant model, derived from analyses of Star Carr, supposes that communities lived in large base camps in winter, and fragmented in the summer, with smaller hunting parties climbing into the hills. In a very important discussion, Penny Spikins has shown

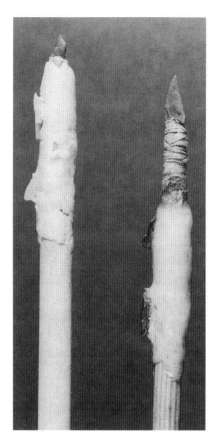

39 Microliths reconstructed as projectile points.
© B. Finlayson

that models of this kind do not deal well with the character of the archaeological record and are founded on a poor understanding of ethnographic examples – what she calls 'ethno-fictions'. All too often the models are too rigid and detailed and small pieces of evidence are used to support and sustain much larger abstractions.

This is very significant because, very often, there is more variation in the evidence than large-scale models allow. One of the striking features of the date from isotope analysis of human bone, for example, is a sense of variation. Samples from the shell midden of Cnoc Coig, Oronsay, indicate a diet with a very heavy reliance on marine sources of protein, and it is argued that this is probably derived from fish and shellfish rather than marine mammals. At Caisteal nan Gillean II, also on Oronsay, and broadly contemporary with Cnoc Coig, the single bone analysed demonstrates a diet of mixed terrestrial and marine protein. This is especially interesting because Oronsay is a tiny island, and there has been a long-running debate about whether a single group stayed on Oronsay all year, moving from midden to midden, or whether they moved from island to island, only occasionally visiting Oronsay. In either case, the variation in diet should be noted.

Slightly further afield, in Ireland, isotope analysis of human bones from two middens shows a further potential complication. Analysis of a thigh bone fragment from a shell midden at Rockmarshall, on the south of the Cooley peninsula in Co. Louth, indicates a mixed diet of terrestrial and marine proteins, whereas a broadly contemporary site at Ferriter's Cove, Co. Kerry, shows a diet heavily dominated by marine resources. Again, the sense is of variation between different sites. Most important, however, is the fact that at Ferriter's Cove the extensive faunal remains on site indicated a mixed diet, with wild boar, a range of fish, probably caught in traps, and shellfish. There are many plausible explanations of these slightly contradictory data: possibly different members of the community ate different diets; possibly the individual with a marine-rich diet was a newcomer to the community, moving in marriage (Rick Schulting has argued that isotope evidence from Brittany demonstrates women moving in marriage from inland to the coast); possibly the bone was that of an ancestor, carried around with a community and only deposited much later, and consequently the link between the diet of the individual and the faunal assemblage is weaker.

Several interpretations of the patterns discussed above are possible, but the example clearly highlights an analytical problem in moving between individuals and sites, as well as in considering the cultural logics that structured the deposition of material in the past. How do we know that a shell midden contains all of the species a community relied upon? What decisions structured the deposition of material into different parts of the landscape? In a broader sense the difficulties in reconciling the analysis of an individual's skeletal remains with the analysis of a mass of faunal data provide a useful reminder of the scales of evidence that archaeological narratives are based upon. Most faunal assemblages (and most lithic scatters) are aggregates of long-term behaviour and it is clear that individuals can vary.

HUNTING AND GATHERING AS WAYS OF PERCEIVING THE ENVIRONMENT

I take my title for this section from a paper by the anthropologist Tim Ingold. He argues that hunting and gathering, and the skills they involve, are not just a way of obtaining resources. Instead Ingold proposes that hunting and gathering are ways of seeing and understanding particular qualities of the world.

Take, for example, the use of chert pebbles by hunter-gatherers in the Upper Tweed Valley, Scottish Borders. In and around the town of Peebles surface collections made by Bob Knox show that many stone tools were made of battered and rolled pebbles of chert, a flint-like material that is quite common in the area. At sites like Manor Bridge and Cavalry Park it seems that, amongst other things, hunter-gatherers were selecting and testing water-rolled pebbles of chert. Sometimes, they just removed a flake or two to test the material, sometimes they worked the pebble fully, transforming it into a core. The point I want to make is simple; for people of the mesolithic in this area, being able to spot a chert pebble on a river side or exposed terrace (*colour plate 12*) was an important skill. In contrast, today most of us would walk straight past a chert pebble, with little thought. The difference is in the ways in which people have learnt to observe different aspects of the world: the ways in which we interact with the world are historically quite specific, and, in turn, these interactions have a huge influence on the ways we understand the world.

Of course this is not just true of the past, but also of today: we view the world in very specific fashions – an archaeologist's eye is different to that of an ecologist. In his book *The Snow Geese* William Fiennes discusses how his new interest in ornithology opens up aspects of the world to him, of which he had never been aware. Birdwatching is not as simple as matching names to shapes, but includes consideration of behaviours, ways of noticing relationships. More than anything, the pleasure lies in time spent intently engaged with an aspect of the world. As he concludes 'learning the names is a method of noticing'. (Fiennes, W. 2002 *The Snow Geese* Picador, p.95). The ways in which we learn to notice aspects of the world are tied up with senses of identity.

Another example of a sensitive reading of the specifics of 'procurement activity' is provided by Tony Pollard's recent discussion of the shell middens of western Scotland. As noted above, shell middens have often been treated as simple reservoirs of information about diet. In a stimulating paper Pollard suggested that evidence from middens suggested the ways in which people's activity was integrated with the rhythms of the tides:

> low tide occurs every day, twice a day, and it is these temporary windows which provide the cue for the intensification of activity on the shore, with people perhaps setting aside other tasks and moving from areas removed from the shore in order to reap the harvest of these temporary forests of kelp and fields of mussels.
> Pollard, T. 1996.

Building on this, Pollard suggests a possible distinction in this area between agriculturalists, for whom time is marked by the sun's movements through the heavens, and hunter-gatherers, for whom the tides, and consequently the moon, were more significant. Further work carried out on middens from Scotland and Ireland has suggested that in some cases, people were exploiting especially low tides at night in order to collect the largest shellfish. This provides a striking image of how people organised their time and how this differs from the ways in which we routinely structure the day. This also provides links to a discussion in the last chapter about how the night provided alternative sources of light (moon, stars and possibly Aurora): the night only appears especially dark to modern city dwellers. Given such differences in their basic routines of life, it is possible that mesolithic people conceived light and dark in very different ways than many people do today.

By thinking carefully about what the archaeological materials mean in terms of people's activities in the past, archaeologists can begin to highlight some interesting specifics about people's lives. For example, work on the shellfish remains from Morton has suggested that these weren't collected from the best possible environments in the vicinity of the site. Instead, Margaret Deith proposes that the main aim of people's journeys was to obtain raw materials to manufacture stone tools: shellfish provided an easy resource to collect on the way home. These examples show some of the ways in which procuring material created complex interlocking webs with other aspects and rhythms of the world, or other tasks that needed to be carried out. These tangled webs would have sustained particular sets of meanings – ideas about the appropriate ways for communities, and the people within them, to behave. Archaeologists have recently become very interested in the ways in which different tasks combine to create a 'taskscape' (see chapter 6).

A final example of the ways in which routine activity and understanding are entwined comes from considering mobility by sea (*colour plate 13*). It is clear from the distribution of sites and differing materials in Scotland that mobility by sea was quite common in the mesolithic. Recent confirmation of mesolithic presence on Orkney and the Western Isles shows that people had crossed the Pentland Firth and the Minch, two of the most dangerous stretches of water in the British Isles. Disturbances to the vegetation sequence at Catta Ness on Shetland have even been interpreted by some specialists as demonstrating that mesolithic people brought deer to the island, in order to provide them with food. This not only suggests a long-distance journey, some 50 miles as the crow flies from the closest part of Orkney, or nearer to 60 if broken by the Fair Isle, but implies that it may have been done with deer in the boat. The cod bones from Morton have been interpreted as indicating offshore fishing, presumably implying some seafaring abilities.

That at least some mesolithic people were adept seafarers is likely from a range of evidence, through direct evidence of boats used is lacking. Finds of logboats have been made from southern Scandinavia; some were used for burials. The boats are often made of lime and include fireplaces and may be associated with finely decorated wooden paddles. In Ireland a possible fragment of a logboat has been found in Lough Neagh, dating to the later part of the mesolithic period. However, in Scotland no definite examples of mesolithic boats are known. A dugout was found on an early peat surface sealed by carse clays at Friarton, Perth. Although now lost, this boat, from an area of known mesolithic finds, may be mesolithic in date. The pine log was 4.5m long, with a burnt-out cavity some 1.8m long and 60cm deep. Chris Smith notes that the geological context of the find is poorly known, and that the size of the cavity suggest that it may not have been a boat at all but, drawing on Scandinavian parallels, possibly a coffin. Other possible, although contentious, examples of logboats have been recorded from carse deposits on the Clyde. A little to the south Richard Chatterton has recently drawn attention to an 1888 find at Hylton, on the River Wear, of a dugout boat with associated material including human bones. Although undated, this has close parallels to the Scandinavian traditions of boat-burials. These varied fragments of evidence suggest that dugout boats were most likely in use during the period, and hint at funerary associations. In this respect, it is important to consider that temperate wood tends to float very high in the water and is rather unstable at sea. Dugouts of these materials would most likely have been used on rivers, or in sheltered estuaries – which is also where they have been found. Skin- or bark-covered boats constructed from wooden frames, similar to Irish currachs or coracles, would, however, have been more seaworthy and it seems likely that something of this type may also have been in use for journeys on the open sea.

Regardless of the kind of boat used, seafaring appears to have been, at least for some people, a quite routine activity. Yet, in a similar way to the absence of woodlands in most narratives, the implications that this routine seafaring had for mesolithic lives has rarely been explored. Moving small boats in sight of land is often called pilotage, and commentators have compared this skill to an 'art'. As I see it, this describes the involvement of individuals and communities within a flow of interpretation and representation of the world around them:

> achievement (in pilotage) depended on handed-on experience, local knowledge and detailed observation of natural phenomena … such as the weather sequences, the tides, the movements of the sun, moon and the stars, and the habits of birds and fish … survival could depend upon perceptive interpretation of these observations and such a body of orally transmitted knowledge was an important aspect of a culture.
> McGrail, S. 1987. *Ancient Boats in north west Europe: the archaeology of water transport to* AD *1500*, Longmans, p.275

Seafaring then, was not just about boats, but about wider bodies of knowledge. The argument that the ways in which people learn to notice aspects of the world is tied up with their senses of identity suggests that for some of the later mesolithic communities of western Scotland paying attention to the sea in particular skilled ways was a key aspect of senses of self (*40*). The engagement of a seafarer with the sea was a truly intimate association. In fact, it is the interplay between individuals and communities, between particular interpretations of the world and the bodies of knowledge characteristic of wider groups, that is of real interest. Bodies of knowledge of this kind were not blindly inherited, as part of an individual's birthright, but were inculcated through practice: skills were both taught and learned and the processes of passing on skills formed a key texture of social life.

Access to the skills surrounding seafaring was probably empowering: it is important to note that not all members of mesolithic communities necessarily had equal opportunity to become skilled seafarers. Splits along gender or age lines are likely. In particular the interplay between the physical demands of seafaring and the experience of interpreting the seas may have been significant. The young maybe could out-row their elders, but could they match their knowledge of the sea's moods? As the years passed perhaps the eyesight of a skilled seafarer would decline, or the arthritis in their joints become too severe to allow long periods of rowing in the harsh salt-spray. Further differentiations within communities are also possible. Boats, be they dugout logs, or skin vessels, were an investment of time and energy and may have involved coordinating labour: this is especially true of dugout boats. It is very likely that not all members of the community owned boats. This is not to assume that all boats had individual owners, many hunter-gatherers and other small-scale communities have different attitudes to property than those of the modern west. Today, many objects are associated with an identifiable owner whereas concepts of communal ownership and belonging are possibly more appropriate for the peoples discussed here. This suggests that boats were woven into complex mosaics of relationships: of who had a claim to use of a boat and at what times. In this context, and thinking more broadly, the use of boats for burials in southern Scandinavia, with a dead person being laid out in a boat, may be a clear manifestation of the link between a person, other members of the community and the ability to create a key aspect of a community's material world. The form of boats themselves may have held many

40 Sea at Aberdeen Bay. © *G. Warren*

complex associations. Chris Tilley, for example, has demonstrated how canoe building on Wala, Malekula, Melanesia, involves articulating competing metaphors and identities, especially those relating to understandings of gender.

Boats were, of course, vital to the lives of the wider community in providing means of transport and for obtaining resources. Moving across the sea, be it to fish for cod, or to collect traps, or simply to visit kin, provided opportunities for different relationships. Boats most likely carried small groups of people from within the community: at times a family, at other times a small task group, heading off to procure some flint, or hunt some boar. These small groups, as they carried out their tasks, most likely came into contact with other groups of foragers: perhaps the smoke from their fires drew them together. Contact with distant kin, or with strangers, provided important contexts in which to maintain and transform relationships of different kinds: to engage in gossip, to arrange marriages, discuss land and sea disputes, hear rumour of the new and talk of the old. Access to this knowledge and these relationships was empowering, and was intimately dependent upon, and associated with, seafaring. Mary Helms has argued persuasively that the ability to travel to and from distant places, and bring news from these places can often be associated with power relationships. In a mesolithic Scottish context there is little clear evidence of unusual materials being brought from distant places (see chapter 7), but such associations may be appropriate.

Working with the sea had its own rhythms. As in the discussion of shell middens, above, seafaring was entwined with the tides. The lunar clock was important in engaging with the sea, especially in assessing how to ride the tides in small craft: when was it safe to set out on a journey; how far could be travelled; how did the stars act as navigation guides? The times of the seasons also impacted on seafaring: the social world expanded in the long days of safe sailing in the summer, and contracted in the stormy dark winter.

Such associations begin to round out notions of seafaring in the mesolithic of Scotland, providing wider frameworks of belief and a context in which biographies extended. Of course, the details are speculative, but the study provides a powerful example of how a simple technology is tied into much broader associations. These arguments can be extended even further. I noted in chapter 2 that sea level change was, at times, rapid, and that seafaring would have involved sailing over the homes of the ancestors: perhaps even where parents had lived. I drew attention to the presence of reworked patinated tools in many coastal mesolithic sites in the region: tools that were recognisably human, but strangely transformed into the colour of bones. In previous discussions of this matter I have speculated on the possible significance of the sea as a home of the ancestors, or an underworld. More concretely, as sea levels rose islands were created where headlands had once been, and as the waters fell islands were joined to the mainland. Again, regardless of the details, it is easy to see how this experience of change must have been a key part of the myths associated with the sea in the mesolithic.

Adding together these sketches provide a sense that the sea was probably central to some mesolithic lives. At one level it provided food and sustenance, but bound together with the need for calories were a series of associations that provided the basic substance of mesolithic life in the area. None of this was set or fixed, but these associations developed through experience, and changed over time. Boats were never just birch bark or deer hide stretched on a frame, nor pine or lime transformed by fire and the blow of an antler axe. Boats were an intimate aspect of the mesolithic world of Scotland, and exploring the fluid associations between these objects, people and landscapes can be very rewarding.

REVIEW

At the outset of this chapter I suggested that archaeological interpretations had often assumed that the procurement of resources was the easiest aspect of mesolithic lives to interpret. In fact, I could have gone further and argued that archaeologists have behaved as if it was the only part of their lives they could think about. Embedded within this are a series of assumptions, including a dichotomy between the technical and the social, as well as many value judgements about diet. A fine-grained focus on the evidence from the mesolithic shows that things were much more complex than archaeologists have sometimes allowed – that ways of getting hold of the materials needed for life helped to create and sustain rich and varied ways of understanding the world. Of course, my discussions here have been limited in scope: I have discussed procuring food and working of stone, and ways of moving. I have not focused on how animals were transformed into bone and antler tools, or their hides into clothing, or sinews and ligaments into cords. I have not examined woodcraft – the selection of materials of differing kinds for different tasks, from fire starting and maintenance through to supports for buildings. Plants in general have remained elusive in these outlines, not least because of preservation biases.

Many of these materials are returned to in the chapters that follow: my hope at this stage is that the examples presented help suggest that a thicker and more contextualised way of considering the procurement of materials brings rewards.

FURTHER READING

A range of literature touches on the key issues discussed in this chapter. Clark (1976) and Finlay (2000) discuss key issues of bias. Hampton's book (1999) on stone tool use includes details of the *bumkil* and Vicky Cumming's paper in a recent edited volume by Rob Young discusses the southern Welsh material. Chatterton's discussion of deposition is in a fine review chapter of evidence for ritual in the British and Irish mesolithic. My own discussion of the skills of seafaring at the time is in the same volume. Schulting and Richards (2000) offer a good introduction to isotope analysis, and have since published many papers on the topic. Richards and Mellars (1998) and Mithen (2000) offer critical discussions of the nature of settlement on Oronsay. Tony Pollard's 'Time and Tide' paper (1996) includes some very fine discussions of shell middens, and Paul Mellar's 1987 account of the Oronsay excavations remains one of the most detailed accounts of a programme of excavations of middens; Russell et al. 1995 offer a detailed account of aspects of shellfish exploitation at Ulva and Pollard et al. review material from a shell midden at Risga, with an interesting account of an early excavation. Milner (forthcoming) offers a wider review of subsistence and other evidence. Bill Finlayson and Steve Mithen discuss use wear in a 1997 paper and in chapters within the Southern Hebrides Mesolithic Project report (Mithen 2000).

Chatterton, R. forthcoming. 'Ritual' in C. Conneller and G. Warren (eds) *Mesolithic Britain and Ireland: new approaches*. (Stroud: Tempus Publishing)

Clark, J.G.D. 1954. 'Excavations at Star Carr : an early mesolithic site at Seamer near Scarborough Yorkshire'. (Cambridge: Cambridge University Press)

Clarke, D.L. 1976. 'Mesolithic Europe: the economic basis' in G. de Sieveking, I.H. Longworth and K.E. Wilson (eds) *Problems in Economic and Social Archaeology*, pp.449-81. (London: Duckworth)

Cummings, V. 2000. 'Myth, Memory and Metaphor: the significance of space, place and landscape in Mesolithic Pembrokeshire' in R. Young (ed.) *Mesolithic Lifeways: current research from Britain and Ireland*, pp.87-96. (Leicester)

Fiennes, W. 2002. *The Snow Geese* Picador, p.95

Finlay, N. 2000. 'Deer Prudence' in *Archaeological Review from Cambridge* 17(1): 67-79

Finlayson, B. and Mithen, S. 1997. 'The microwear and morphology of microliths from Gleann Mor' in Knecht (ed.) *Projectile Technology*, pp.107-129. (New York/London: Plenum press)

Hampton, O.B. 1999. *Culture of Stone: Sacred and Profane Uses of Stone among the Dani*. (Texas: A&M)

Mellars, P.A. 1987 *Excavations on Oronsay*. (Edinburgh)

Milner, N. forthcoming. 'Subsistence' in C. Conneller and G. Warren (eds) *Mesolithic Britain and Ireland: new approaches*. (Stroud: Tempus Publishing)

Mithen, S.J. 2000 'Hunter-gatherer landscape archaeology: The Southern Hebrides Mesolithic Project 1988-98'. (Cambridge: McDonald Institute Monographs)

Mithen, S.J. 2000. 'Mesolithic sedentism on Oronsay: chronological evidence from adjacent islands in the southern Hebrides' in *Antiquity* 74: 298-304

Pollard, T. 1996. 'Time and Tide: Coastal Environments, Cosmology and Ritual Practice in Early Prehistoric Scotland' in T. Pollard and A. Morrison (eds) *The Early Prehistory of Scotland*, 198-210. (Edinburgh: Edinburgh University Press)

Pollard, T., Atkinson, J., and Banks, I. 1996. 'It is the technical side of the work which is my stumbling block: a shell midden site on Risga reconsidered' in T. Pollard and A. Morrison (eds) *The Early Prehistory of Scotland*, 165-182. (Edinburgh: Edinburgh University Press)

Richards, M.P. and Mellars, P.A. 1998. 'Stable isotopes and the seasonality of the Oronsay middens' in *Antiquity* 72: pp.178-84

Russell, N.J., Bonsall, C. and Sutherland, D.G. 1995. 'The role of shellfish gathering in the Mesolithic of western Scotland: the evidence from Ulva Cave' in A. Fischer (ed.) *Man and Sea in the Mesolithic*, pp.273-288. (Oxford: Oxbow)

Schulting, R.J. and Richards, M.P. 2000. 'The use of stable isotopes in studies of subsistence and seasonality in the British mesolithic' in R. Young (ed.) *Mesolithic Lifeways: current research from Britain and Ireland*, 55- 66. (Leicester)

Spikins, P. 2000. 'Ethno-facts or Ethno-fiction? Searching for the structure of settlement patterns' in R. Young (ed.) *Mesolithic Lifeways: current research from Britain and Ireland*, 105-118. (Leicester)

Warren, G.M. 2000. 'Seascapes: peoples, boats and inhabiting the later mesolithic in western Scotland' in R. Young (ed.) *Mesolithic Lifeways: current research from Britain and Ireland*, 97-104. (Leicester)

AN INTERJECTION

You've mentioned that many accounts of hunter-gatherers have tended to be large scale, or concerned with ecology. I can see what you're trying to do by focusing on people and how they made sense of the world, but people had to survive over the long term; in a broad sense, they must have adapted to the environment. Surely it is this long-term view that's more important.

It depends what you're asking. I've been a bit disingenuous, and haven't really been fair to the diversity of ways in which archaeologists and anthropologists have made sense of hunter-gatherers. In particular, there are recent approaches that explicitly attempt to understand hunter-gatherer activity as a result of environmental factors. One example is 'behavioural ecology'. In this kind of intellectual framework hunting for different species (or gathering other resources, although its mainly hunting they talk about) is understood in terms of benefits and penalties accruing in pursuit and capture. Optimal foraging theory, for example, takes an explicitly economic approach to questions of hunter-gatherer behaviour, comparing energy gained and expended in the search for resources, arguing that such behaviour must be efficient or else the forces of evolution would select other alternatives. Some of these accounts are interesting, but behavioural ecological explanations, at their most extreme, offer an exceptionally mechanistic view of hunter-gatherer behaviour: hunting decisions are to do with the input of calories, or that male hunting is a way of showing prowess and thus gaining access to sexually receptive females. Behavioural ecologists accept that contemporary hunter-gatherers do not really think in this way about their actions, but would argue that the explanations given by hunter-gatherers are only *proximate* causes or arguments. In contrast the behavioural ecologist offers an *ultimate* (i.e. evolutionary) explanation for their activity.

I'm not sure that we need to accept this kind of approach, and the more time I've spent looking at the mesolithic of Britain and Ireland the harder I've found it to reconcile its diversity with these kind of generalising models. Questions of analytical scale are vital to any archaeology, but are perhaps especially so in a period like the mesolithic, where we have a fragmentary data set, and long time periods.

So surely the better approach is the long term one?

Not necessarily. It all depends what you are trying to argue, and what you are building from. My focus here is fine-grained, not least because I still don't understand some of the details – why people chose to deposit material in particular places, for example. I don't feel happy about working at the larger scales until I can get these issues resolved. As I argued earlier, many large-scale models, those systems that I discussed earlier, are built on a series of fairly simple assumptions about how hunter-gatherers behave. I think they have potential to be very misleading. Therefore, at this stage, I think the best approach is to try and better understand the intimate details of mesolithic archaeology.

5

CRAFT AND SKILL

Examining the ways in which the procurement of resources was connected to perceptions of the world begins to break down traditional views of hunter-gatherer subsistence activity as a solely economic practice. Instead, in the previous chapter thinking about subsistence practices and routines of movement provided some sense of the conditions within which people came to know the world. In this chapter I extend these arguments through an examination of the production of artefacts. As I have argued, frequently, archaeologists have seen artefacts in a fairly straightforward, functional way. Alongside this, the actual form of artefacts is often supposed to derive from the interplay of practical need and a tradition of making things in particular ways. Participation in a tradition of making, choosing for example to make microliths of a certain shape, is often seen as indicating a shared background linking an individual to a wider group. This is often described as a 'cultural' heritage. This perception of the manufacture of objects being influenced by a cultural heritage is slightly problematic. In much the same way that I argued one must think of the skills associated with seafaring being learnt through practice and experience, rather than being a birthright, I argue in this chapter that archaeologists need to rethink understandings of manufacture and use of materials in the past. This is especially important today, as very few people are actively concerned with the manufacture of objects as part of their daily lives and the skills and knowledge involved in such acts are at some distance from many people's experience.

A useful start is provided by using the word 'craft' to think about the ways people made things. In the conception outlined above 'craft' implies little more than the manifestation of a tradition or cultural heritage. The individuals involved in craft activities are therefore empty vessels, reiterating the actions dictated by their culture. There is no sense in this kind of account that people in the past were skilled practitioners and that ways of doing things were closely tied up in ways of understanding the world. Skilled craft episodes were influenced by contexts and decisions, by the kinds of projects that people were involved in, or the materials they had to hand. Yet it is precisely this sense of skilled engagement that comes from the ethnographic literature and from our own experiences in our everyday lives in a variety of contexts, not just acts of manufacture. It is worth reiterating that mesolithic people had the same cognitive potentials as we do. To ignore such complexity in archaeological accounts is therefore to downplay the humanity of our subjects. In a stimulating discussion Francis Spufford has argued that polar explorers' understandings of Inuit technology in the nineteeth and early twentieth century allowed little space for thinking about native skill and ability. Instead, technology was seen as an adaptation to an extreme environment, and driven entirely by this environment. White explorers could gain these skills through learning (although many did not bother, and died as a consequence) – but for the Inuit learning and development was not an option: their skills were determined by the landscape. Thus an understanding of technology and skill facilitated an ideology of domination – what Spufford describes as Borealism. All too often archaeological accounts of mesolithic skills and craft fall into a similar trap.

So perhaps the focus should be upon craft as involving invention, instability and change – people in the past as actively reinventing their material culture, dynamically driving the development of technology. Well, this would not do either. For it is clear that there are large-scale spatial and temporal similarities in material culture during the

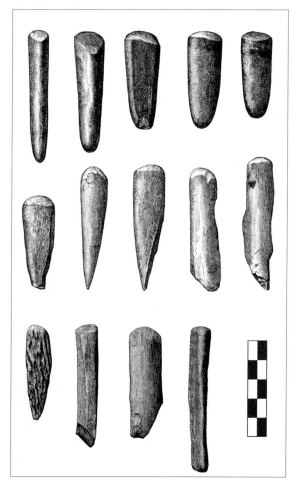

41 Bevel-ended tools. Upper and middle rows: Caisteal nan Gillean, Oronsay. Lower row: Macarthur Cave, Oban. Left: Druimvargie Cave, Oban; centre and right: Macarthur Cave, Oban. Reproduced at 1:2. *After Anderson 1895 Figs 5 & 8, and Anderson 1898 Figs 19-28*

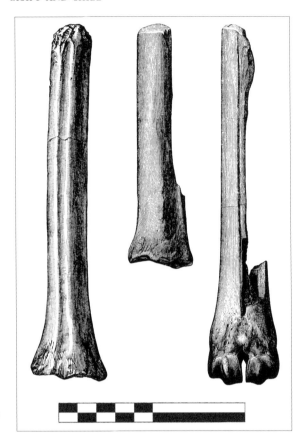

42 Bevel-ended tools. Left:
Druimvargie Cave, Oban. Centre
and right: Macarthur Cave, Oban.
Reproduced at 1:2. *After Anderson 1895
Figs 9 & 10, and Anderson 1898 Fig 8*

mesolithic period in Europe, and these simply cannot result from fortuitous reinventions. In fact, what is required in our analysis is a way of understanding the interplay between long-lived traditions of craft and the potential for variation that always existed. Due to its preservation, stone offers the dominant archaeological resource for the mesolithic period, and much of this chapter is devoted to it.

NETWORKS

Individual actions of craft clearly formed part of much wider chains of activity stretching through communities and across the landscape. Acts such as the procurement of resources, the construction of artefacts, or the deposition of debris formed the fabric of people's lives, and the ways in which they were interwoven with other tasks was historically specific and a key aspect of identity. This notion of interlocking activities is what the anthropologist Tim Ingold calls a 'taskscape', and recent years have seen some archaeological interest in how the taskscape allows a more social perspective on early prehistory. In particular, archaeologists interested in material culture, such as Chantal Conneller, have explored the ways in which the manufacture of stone tools was structured across the landscape, and involved relationships and obligations between people that extended across space (*colour plate 14*). As such, every artefact can be thought of as being embedded in networks linking them to other places and times. The character of these networks is manifested in the physical form of artefacts. Therefore, attempting to reconstruct them by exploding artefacts back out to their relationships across the landscape, offers a way of identifying the possibilities for social relationships. A good example is provided by one of the simplest artefacts in northern British prehistory: the bevel-ended tool (*41* and *42*).

Bevel-ended tools of stone, antler and bone are found throughout Britain, Ireland and into Brittany. These are elongated tools with a pronounced bevel (or two bevels) present at one, or sometimes both ends, sometimes in association with small flake scars: there is debate about whether the scars represent flaking in use or shaping of tips; likewise, whether the bevel simply results from use, or is deliberately pre-shaped is also questioned. Bone and antler examples are almost entirely restricted to middens, whereas stone bevel-ended tools are found more widely. Large numbers of bevel-ended tools are found on some sites: over 150 in the MacArthur Cave, Oban, for example. Direct radiocarbon dates on organic bevel-ended tools in Scotland show a long currency of use; from the mesolithic into the Bronze Age.

Discussion has long focused on function, with bevel-ended tools sometimes interpreted as limpet hammers or scoops, sometimes as flint working tools, sometimes as leather working tools. Experimental work has been carried out on a number of occasions, with conflicting results. There is little clear consensus, reflecting the probability that even this simple tool had differing functions in prehistory. It is interesting that the physical properties of bone, antler and stone are very different; antler, for example, is a resilient material, that deals much better with impacts than bone, stone is harder than both. Whatever use(s) bevel-ended tools were put to it seems likely that the choice of raw material was deliberate and it is not clear that bone, antler and stone tools were used for the same purposes.

Regardless of their use, bevel-ended tools reveal complex networks. For a start, the provision of raw materials for these objects was far from straightforward. Much of the stone was presumably available from local beach sources, and is relatively uninformative, but the bone and antler examples help flesh out something of the scheduling of the taskscape.

The faunal assemblage from varied Oronsay middens in the fifth millennium BC indicates the importation to the island of raw materials for tool manufacture, in the form of the lower limbs of red deer, shed and unshed antler. A similar pattern was found at Sand, Inner Sound, in the seventh millennium BC implying some stability in demands on people's routines. Bone bevel-ended tools are manufactured mainly on red deer metapodial (lower limb) bones, despite a wider range of species being available, implying some deliberate choice. The use of shed antler is also interesting: in 1555 Olaus Magnus noted that it was as easy to see hinds calve as to find shed antlers: implying searches across the landscape for this raw material. Today red deer sometimes eat shed antler. Bone and antler bevel-ended tools are sometimes made of fragments of larger tools, often assumed to have broken and been recycled: at MacArthur's Cave, Oban, three bevel-ended forms were manufactured on fragments of barbed points.

The details of manufacture are controversial but may have involved soaking of antler, and certainly involved other materials: hammer stones, wedges and abrasives, all of which required procurement themselves. Thus the simple bevel-ended tool carries implications across the mesolithic landscape implying butchery sites or long searches for antler; the curation of fragmentary tools to be reworked into bevel-ended tools; the selection of material and, possibly, manufacture of handles. All of these networks of activity must have been intermeshed with other projects, and the details of their scheduling formed an essential context within which people came to know the world. These contexts themselves were reproduced over time by the actions of mesolithic people, and the effective reproduction of these patterns of behaviour season after season, generation after generation, led to the palimpsest sites that so dominate the mesolithic archaeological record.

These discussions highlight that individual artefacts have implications across the landscape as a whole. Examining the nature of mesolithic flint assemblages in eastern Scotland also provides clear evidence of networks linking different places. In this area flint is mainly available as cobbles on the beaches, and considering where different stages in the transformation of a cobble into a blade or microlith took place is rewarding. At Castle Street, Inverness for example, in an assemblage based on the exploitation of beach pebble flint, the initial phases of working pebbles – removing its coarse outer cortex or skin and beginning to shape a core – are not present, but there is substantial evidence for the manufacture of blades and flakes. This indicates the movement of prepared cores to and from the location. To the south, at the Sands of Forvie, there is great evidence for preparation of cores (*colour plate 15*) and production of blades and microliths, most of which were removed from the site (see also *11*). In Aberdeen three small mesolithic sites have been excavated. At this time Aberdeen was probably a varied, rich environment, with low gravel hills rising above mires and estuarine channels. The sites are small, that at St Paul Street is interpreted as a single occupation on the basis of the presence of all stages of reduction, and the possible presence of a hearth. The largest assemblage is from The Green, and consists of only 297 pieces. James Kenworthy suggests that the assemblage was produced over a short time period by one person, and that it most likely involved maintenance of tools. At Fife Ness a small assemblage in association with a light structure in a coastal location has few cores, and little débitage. Tool use appears to be indicated, with manufacture taking place elsewhere.

These technical networks linking sites are also evidenced in the north of Scotland, where Meli Pannett has demonstrated pre-preparation of cores on the shores, and a very low representation of cores inland. The patterns in Aberdeenshire appear to be very similar. Further west, the Southern Hebrides Mesolithic Project has also identified the movement of raw materials and artefacts across the landscape, including caches of flints at Staosnaig and partially worked cores at a number of sites. Similar patterns are also evidenced in a different technological tradition in Ireland.

The evidence suggests that the organisation of stone-tool manufacture across the landscape was complex and carefully structured. It is important to note that these networks provided powerful links between differing sites, and between the coastal and inland areas. Structuring of artefact production and use in this way implies planning of movements between places. It also, of course, involves negotiation of differing demands upon time.

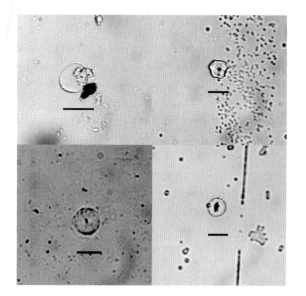

Above left: 43 Starch grains extracted from the edges of stone tools from the Sands of Forvie, Aberdeenshire. Top left: sub-ovate starch grain and cellulose tissue. Scale bar 25μ. Top right: polygonal starch grain. Scale bar 15μ. Bottom left: Spherulite. Scale bar 15μ. Bottom right: round starch grain. Scale bar 10μ. © *G. Warren*

Above right: 44 Reconstructed fish trap at Archaeolink, Aberdeenshire. © *G. Warren*

At the Sands of Forvie, for example, the lithic evidence clearly suggests the production of material to be carried away from the site across the landscape. Forvie is a place where stone-tool manufacturing takes place in advance of other tasks – a place where these activities are anticipated and planned. Yet there is also evidence from functional analysis for substantial amounts of plant working using stone tools at Forvie. Microscopic examination of patterns of damage on flint tools, and analysis of starch grains adhering to the tools (*43*) indicates a range of activities involving starchy plants. Little attention has been focused on the production of the means of procurement of marine resources in mesolithic Scotland. Although analyses of faunal remains have sometimes identified inshore or offshore fishing, sometimes with traps, the manufacture of the items needed for such fishing has been little discussed. This leads to a strange lacuna in accounts of the organisation of mesolithic lives – the vast quantities of time that must have been expended in the production of organic material culture (for example, *44*). The production of as vital a piece of equipment as string has remained almost entirely absent from discussions of the mesolithic in Scotland, for example. It is possible that the large quantity of plant working at Forvie indicates that it was also a place to prepare such equipment. Forvie was most likely a ridge located above a salt marsh with plentiful reeds and grasses – ideal materials for the production of string (*45*). (Of course, some, at least, of the processing of plants was presumably tied into other tasks: preparing of food, clothing or medicines.) Thus Forvie may have been a location where tool preparation of varied kinds took place both in stone, which commonly dominates the evidence, and in other materials, which survive much less often. Forvie also shows the importance of tools being used simply to make other tools. The networks that formed the taskscape were complex, and involved competing demands.

The existence of these networks lying behind individual artefacts offers some indication of why long-term similarities in material culture might exist: a decision to change had implications beyond a single moment and, as argued in the last chapter, all kinds of seemingly mundane activities were tied up in complex understandings of the world including symbolic beliefs. Recent experimental work examining the persistence of formal types over time has also indicated that this is much more successful if they have a shared meaning and are not simply reproduced as abstract shapes or forms. In this regard, it is interesting that for some, although by no means all, small-scale traditional societies, an important aim is to live in the appropriate, or the correct way – often one that has been mapped out by the ancestors. Barry Lopez, for example, argues that 'the great task of life for the traditional Eskimo is still to achieve congruence with a reality which is already given'. (Lopez, B. 1986. *Arctic Dreams: imagination and desire in a northern landscape*, Harvill, p.411). This includes marrying the activities of life with all of the other aspects of the world, including the spiritual. Sometimes such 'traditional' societies are described as 'cold' societies, with the implication that they have exhibited little historical change, in contrast to 'hot' modern societies, with our breathless cult of the new. Marek Zvelebil, for instance, has argued that the traditional outlook of European mesolithic communities manifested itself in long-term stabilities. These arguments are interesting, but it is not always clear what kinds of ideas are tied up with productive acts – discussions of these processes all too often lack detail. Recent re-examinations of the production of stone tools, and especially microliths, are relevant in this regard.

MICROLITHS IN THE MAKING

This subtitle is taken from an article by Nyree Finlay, published in 2000. Part of Finlay's research has involved examining the ways in which microliths are caught up in the ways archaeologists talk about mesolithic lives. The microlith is the predominant symbol of the mesolithic in most of north-western Europe (even if there are areas, such as Ireland, where it was not used for long periods of the mesolithic). As outlined above, a microlith is a retouched fragment of a flint blade, made to a reasonably distinctive size and shape (*colour plate 16*). Microlith manufacture involves a series of steps: firstly selection of raw material is undertaken, and a core is prepared from this material; blades are then removed from this core; a blade is then selected and snapped, sometimes with a distinctive notch being worked into the blade in order to weaken it and help determine the angle of snap. The small fragment of blade remaining may then have more of its sides retouched in order to complete the artefact. As discussed earlier, the microlith was traditionally seen as an armature for projectiles, and its form was taken to indicate some kind of particular

45 Reconstruction of a mesolithic plant processing area based on material recovered from the Sands of Forvie, Aberdeenshire. © *A. Braby*

cultural tradition. The different shapes of microliths were even considered to mark boundaries between groups of people across Europe. I have already highlighted that some aspects of this discussion are misplaced: microliths had multiple use, they were not simply projectile points. Finlay's work, which has included experimental manufacture of microliths and placing them in hafts to make compound tools, provides another series of ways of thinking about this key archaeological symbol.

The idea that microliths might be an emblem of affiliation to a particular social, economic or even ethnic group seems tempting at first. But microliths are tiny and, when in use, would have been hafted, leaving just the cutting edge showing. It is striking that most archaeological classification has focused on the size and shape of the blunted edge – exactly the bit that is often hidden when the artefact is hafted. If group identities were signalled through the explicit use of material culture then it seems much more likely that the tool as a whole (the knife, the grater, the fishing spear) carried that message, rather than the small stone tools embedded within it. In this, as in so much else, the preservation qualities of stone have subtly biased constructions of prehistoric lives.

In any case, work carried out by Finlay and her colleague Bill Finlayson, examining microliths from sites in the Inner Hebrides, has shown that the clearly defined archaeological types (scalene triangles, backed blades, rods etc.) merge into one another. Furthermore, the particular 'type' of microlith does not equate with a particular 'type' of use – as discussed in the last chapter not all scalene triangles are used for one thing, and all backed blades for another. In fact, microscopic use wear analysis, combined with detailed characterisations of the morphology of the microliths showed that small morphological details were the important factors in determining use, rather than the overall, archaeologically defined, type.

So where does this leave the interest in microlith manufacture and use? Seemingly the types of microliths bear a problematic relationship to any kind of task people were undertaking, nor can they really be seen as a deliberate indication of cultural background – and in any case, it is possible that archaeological 'types' don't bear any simple relationship to types that may have been recognised in the past. It therefore seems that microliths never deliberately signalled identity in an emblematic way. However, the possibility remains that the ways in which people learnt to make microliths, and other stone tools, would be an interesting area of analysis. Crucially, this discussion moves away from the notion of microlith as symbolic of the mesolithic and towards an understanding of the microlith as part of complex social processes of learning and doing. This returns us to the questions that began the chapter: how does a tradition of craft manifest itself in people?

Most of the time archaeologists have thought of a 'template' carried in people's heads, which they then try and replicate during acts of manufacture. But how do people attain this template? It seems unlikely that people are born with it, as if it was some kind of genetic inheritance. More likely, as people grow up, they come to learn particular ways of making things. The archaeological stress on templates may therefore be misleading, because whilst learning to make particular shaped things is important, learning particular skills and routines of manufacture is surely more significant. To take an extreme example; if someone was to give you a block of flint, a variety of hammers, and a picture of a scalene triangle, it is very likely that you would struggle to manufacture a perfect scalene. Spending time with a skilled practitioner who is engaged in manufacturing microliths may be more useful than a 'template'.

A stress on templates actually deflects analytical attention from a key aspect of social life – the ways in which we learn to manipulate the material world around us in socially acceptable ways. Not by blind replication, nor limitless experiments, but a guided process of apprenticeship – sometimes formal, sometimes not. The reproduction of social *mores* is the basic achievement of any society; and in many hunter-gatherer groups is intimately connected to the character of daily life. Considering social reproduction, in turn, enables us to think about mesolithic people in greater detail. Learning to make things should be key to analysis, not hidden behind a template.

With this in mind, the making of microliths becomes central. Finlay's experimental work has shown that microlith manufacture itself involves a 'sleight of hand' in that certain parts of the process happen, very literally, in the palm of the hand and are hard to observe. Exact formal shapes can only be seen after the craft act. The replication of these objects then involves reusing the same skills and routines of movement, time after time. It involves learning those skills, with attendant trials and experimentation. At Coulerarach, on Islay, Finlay has argued that the lithic assemblage shows a large amount of experimentation, and novice's mistakes – perhaps good evidence of exactly this process of learning.

Thinking about the context of microlith production opens up a whole series of possibilities for engaging with mesolithic lives. Finlay has been critical of assumptions that one person is often perceived to have made and used any given microlith – and, frequently, archaeological assumptions have been that the person is male. She points out that microliths must have been used as part of composite tools, and that this offers the opportunity for many different people's labour to have been brought together. One ethnographically observed example is the grater board: a decorated wooden board with hundreds or thousands of stone chips embedded in it, and used for processing starchy tubers. The boards are a product of women's and men's labour. The former work stone, embed the chip and place red pigment on the board, the latter collect raw materials, carve the board, and after its production is complete, decorate it. The finished board thus embodies the bringing together of different people (and the decorations include totemic animals, suggesting the links between technology and cosmology) and using the board was a reminder of these relationships. Although the grater itself might not be appropriate for mesolithic Scotland the idea of 'multiple authorship' is of considerable importance for rethinking microliths. As Finlay argues, composite tools are labour intensive, but they offer the possibility of integrating different peoples labour into one item:

> There is something quite explicit about the reliance on small microlithic elements in the Mesolithic. Multiplicity is implicit in microlith manufacture and explicit in terms of the hafted component. Because of its reliance and emphasis on multiple components, microlithic technology can be seen as a forum for group participation and expression rather than individual action…'
> Finlay, N. 2003.

STONE WORKING AS A FORM OF KNOWLEDGE

The discussion of microliths demonstrates the complexity and skills apparent in prehistoric craft. Rather than simply replicating a technology, or freely inventing new ways, making an object for a task involved negotiation. People had learnt to work materials in certain ways, and to make certain types of things. Perhaps also this way of thinking about skills and learning helps explain some of the fuzziness of the formal categories discussed above.

On Islay, for example, Finlay demonstrated that scalene triangles at Bolsay Farm were manufactured by retouching the left and distal (furthest from where the hammer struck) parts of a blade (12). At all other sites in the region scalenes were manufactured by retouching the right and proximal ends (closest to where the hammer struck). The two ways of manufacturing create identical artefacts, and she suggested these represent different traditions of working. These patterns suggest some level of intra-regional differentiation in traditions of working. Stepping away from stone tools, Bill Finlayson has argued that bone bevel-ended tools from Morton, Fife, are manufactured in different ways to those on the west coast; again indicating a broad distinction in ways of manufacturing very similar material.

At the Sands of Forvie analyses by Chantal Conneller and myself have demonstrated another range of working traditions. Here a series of concentrations of material are, at one level, all fairly similar, being concerned with the production of blades and microliths. But a detailed analysis demonstrates subtle discriminations between scatters in the ways in which blades were struck. These differences relate to differing levels of skill but more

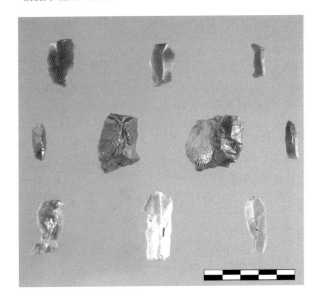

46 Blades and cores from Manor Bridge, Scottish Borders. Scale bar at 1cm intervals. © G. Warren

likely reflect decisions in the past; to work flint more or less carefully for example. However, there are such similarities between other aspects of the scatters that it seems as if people are trying to do things in the same way, but are bringing with them subtle differences, possibly little more than ways of holding their body when working stone: things that they may not have been aware of but that leave traces in the archaeological record. This suggests that as well as intra-regional distinctions in ways of undertaking stone-tool production archaeologists can also think of differences between people in particular places.

And yet, alongside these variations, notwithstanding my argument that prehistoric craft is not a simple manifestation of a tradition, nor a technologically determined response to an environment, one of the most striking facts about the mesolithic period is the persistence of certain material forms across wide geographical areas and over the long term. In Britain generally, the chronological fix on the mesolithic is not great, but it appears that geometric, narrow blade microliths, were in use for the better part of 4000 years. (Some analysts have identified trends over time in these industries, for example for greater use of rods in more recent industries, but this is still somewhat up for debate.) Taken at face value, this longevity of a stone crafting technique implies successful reproduction over time of particular ways of working: this in turn is evidence of success in one of the key challenges faced by any community – the reproduction of particular social values and routines over time, 'social reproduction'. As I argued earlier, most archaeological explanations of this duration would stress the replication of tradition, or argue that the technology was an ecological adaptation. In this final section I would like to suggest that craft skills were deeply embedded with wider understandings of the ways in which the world worked, including many relationships that might be dismissed as spiritual. Aspects of this argument have been made above, with respect to microliths. My aim here is to encompass stone craft more generally.

The production of blades from carefully prepared cores of flint, chert or other materials (46), is characteristic of much of the mesolithic in Scotland and most of the rest of northern Europe. (It should be pointed out that there is much debate about what happens towards the end of the mesolithic, especially in the west of Scotland, with some people arguing that microliths fall out of use, and that a less structured flake industry replaces a blade industry). The dominance of blades has often been interpreted as a reflection of a predominantly mobile lifestyle – blade manufacture is a very efficient way of using stone. There is probably some truth in this explanation, but it fails to deal with several aspects of the evidence.

Firstly, blade industries are found almost regardless of raw material availability. In the south of England, for example, flint sources are much more common, and include larger objects, than the varied stone sources available in many parts of Scotland. Yes, Scottish blades tend to be a bit smaller than their counterparts in England, but the variation in raw material is so much that it seems hard to believe that efficiency alone is the driving force for this persistence.

Secondly many archaeologists argue that as the mesolithic progresses hunter-gatherers become more and more sedentary. If raw material use were solely related to mobility this change would imply transformations in traditions of working. Although there are changes in the use of raw materials between the early and late mesolithic, with the latter seeing a greater use of local raw materials, this is often understood in terms of smaller 'territories' – and in any case blades persist.

Thirdly, the stress on efficiency for blades, although helpful in part, fails to engage with a vital aspect of the material – the aesthetics of blade production. Fine pyramidal blade cores, found throughout the country, are an exceptionally attractive item, many have been worked to small sizes, but retain a delicacy and symmetry. Of course, this is a subjective assessment based on aesthetics, and it is important to remember that many blade cores are scrappy. But the nagging sense persists that there is something about the persistence of blade working that goes beyond the simply functional, efficient explanation. An alternative way of thinking about this problem is to consider stone working as a form of knowledge. I begin by examining the raw materials themselves.

For many communities who work stone on an intimate basis the stone itself is considered to have important spiritual qualities. Some types of stone can be considered to be spiritually charged, or even dangerous. The best-known examples are the aboriginal communities of Australia for whom stone working is inseparable from their understanding of 'the Dreamtime'. The Dreamtime is the basic creation narrative of aboriginal communities, which refers to a time when ancestors walked the land. As the ancestors walked the land they engaged in particular tasks – hunting, fighting, lovemaking – the traces of which form parts of the landscape. Thus a waterhole might have been created by the actions of an ancestor with a digging stick. For many aboriginal societies raw materials are the personification of ancestral forces and the correct use of stone involves negotiating these forces and using them to your best advantage. Quartzite in Arnhemland, for example, is the petrified bones of the ancestors, a spiritually charged material appropriate for manufacturing hunting weapons. The quartzite is a glittery,

47 Dryburgh Mains, Scottish Borders. The ploughed fields shown here are one of the largest mesolithic sites in Scotland, with many thousands of pieces of worked chert, flint and other materials found over the last century. The view is from the high bluffs to the north of the site, looking towards the Eildons.
© G. Warren

iridescent material – properties that the local communities believe to be powerful in any case. In another example the raw material is considered to be semen spilt on the land by the ancestors. Understandings of stone sources are not always as colourful as this. For other communities there is less explicit symbolism attached to stone. For the Wola, agriculturalists of Highland Papua New Guinea, for example, sources for chipped stone are abundant, and there are few explicit symbolic associations. Nevertheless, men habitually say a refrain followed by a whistle when working stone. Some people of the eastern Papuan Highlands believe that the process of stone craft is to release the quality of the tool held within the rock.

The point is not to say that mesolithic Scotland was like Australia at one extreme or Papua New Guinea at the other, but simply to broaden the range of possibilities. The ethnographic accounts of stone working suggest that stone craft and stone sources are always tied up in a particular regime of meaning – or a particular form of knowledge. For many small-scale societies, these associations link people and many other aspects of their environment: stone is only a part of their relational epistemologies. Perhaps then, the mesolithic inhabitants of Scotland came to know the raw materials that surrounded them through such wider bodies of knowledge. Learning to work stone involved not only a physical negotiation of the properties of the raw material, but also a relationship with its spiritual aspects. It is worth considering the ways in which blade working, as an appropriate way of treating material, was embedded in these relationships. The persistence of ways of working stone may, in part, indicate the persistence of local knowledge about the world.

This may have been particularly significant in areas of diverse raw materials, such as the Tweed Valley. Here three main sources of rock were used: chert, chalcedony and flint (colour plate 10). These three materials are visually very distinctive, and were probably found in different parts of the landscape. Chert is abundant in the Upper Tweed, outcropping frequently, and possibly quarried in the period. Flint is presumably derived from beach pebble sources and the chalcedony is probably derived from the Cheviots although pebbles may have been present in the Ettrick and Lower Tweed. It seems likely that these different materials, with their differing origins and physical properties, were understood in different ways. The two largest sites in the region, Rink

Farm and Dryburgh Mains (47), demonstrate similarities between the ways in which the different raw materials were used, implying that particular forms of knowledge about appropriate ways to act in the world were also produced at these sites through particular forms of practice with materials. At both sites cores of the locally abundant chert are dominant, with flint and rare chalcedony also present. Chert shows the interplay between individuals and traditions of working: chert cores are highly varied on both sites, within common limits. Flint was used to exhaustion on both sites – second or third platforms being added to small cores in order to maximise the number of removals possible from the material (platforms, as discussed earlier, are prepared surfaces where a blow will fall in order to remove flakes). Flint cores ended their life smashed between a hammer and an anvil (known as 'bipolar' working) in order to obtain final small flakes. Chalcedony cores with only one platform at both Dryburgh and Rink Farm are quite often regular in form, very attractive cores, not least because of the striking orange, white and purple colours of this material. Two platform cores in chalcedony, however, are more varied in type, and in contrast to flint cores, where a second or third platform was added to maximise the number of removals from a piece of flint, chalcedony cores with two platforms often weigh more than those with one: it seems as if the second platform here is because of a need to maximise removals of a particular size. The differing physical properties of flint, chert and chalcedony are reflected in these decisions about how to structure core and blade production, but the similarities between the sites are unlikely to have arisen by chance. Further similarities in these structures of working can be seen in numerous small surface collections throughout the region. The example therefore demonstrates how particular forms of practice, and assumedly associated beliefs and understandings, were replicated across space and time.

In order to understand how this is possible archaeologists need to think more critically about the contexts within which stone working activities, and particularly apprenticeships, took place. Here the data is a little ambiguous, but in many instances, stone working appears in and around other structural evidence. At sites such as Fife Ness, Morton and in Aberdeen, stone working seems to have taken place next to either light shelters or fires, which have often been interpreted in terms of small family or task groups. At Rum, lithics were demonstrably absent from areas away from the structural evidence. Assuming that many of these structures are 'settlements' (see chapter 6) this implies that some stone working was a part of daily routines. At Forvie, for example, microwear analysis indicates that flint working took place alongside many other tasks, including the processing of plant materials. This daily character of stone working offered continual reiterations of particular ways of doing things, and, following on from the discussion of multiple authorship earlier, also provided ways of maintaining relationships with people. Learning to work stone may have initially taken place by observation within small family or task groups, and would have provided a powerful mechanism for stabilising forms of knowledge about the world.

Yet the emphasis on the immediate small group is not sufficient. For the persistence in stone craft that I have been discussing goes beyond the family or the task group. As discussed, Rink Farm and Dryburgh Mains, on the Tweed are both very large scatters

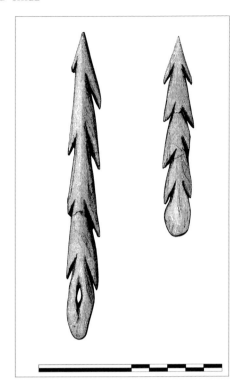

48 Barbed points of antler from the MacArthur's Cave, Oban. Reproduced at 1:2. *After Anderson 1895 Figs 11 & 12*

of worked stone in prime locations. Both include a diverse range of raw material and objects, including chipped and ground stone. As I have already argued, one way of explaining some of the diversity of raw material is to see these sites as locations for larger aggregations of the community, possibly supported by the abundance of salmon. As people journeyed to these sites they carried material for exchange with them. Activity in these places involved a much larger audience than at other times. Stories could be exchanged and deals established. As raw materials changed hands so did aspects of knowledge about the world and people's places within it. Stone working took place in great quantity at these sites, perhaps providing a context within which people saw that their ways of behaving were those of their wider community. It is speculative, but interesting, to consider that some of the working here was undertaken *with* an audience, and with story. In this regard recent work by Meli Pannett at Oliclett, Caithness, is very interesting. Pannett has argued that a series of short-lived, microlith-manufacturing sites are significant as a place in the landscape where it was appropriate to manufacture microliths, set aside from other camps in the area and, at the same time, where the stories and knowledge surrounding this process were learnt.

Of course, the details of these processes elude us. But considering stone working as a form of knowledge, and then considering the ways in which these crafts and skills were reproduced over time provides a much more rounded account of the persistence of types over time. The functional efficiency of blade working was probably significant, but these ways of working stone were embedded in wider bodies of knowledge, and it was the persistence of these bodies of knowledge that led to the distributions of material that archaeologists now discuss.

REVIEW

This chapter has focused on how the manufacture of material culture in the past tied into wider sets of understandings. I suggested that the reasons for people making particular types of artefacts are unclear in most archaeological accounts; explanations are offered at the broadest of scales, but it is not always clear how these operated at the level of the individual craftsperson undertaking a task. Through the examples offered here I have demonstrated that acts of craft have to be understood as part of wider sets of relationships. Some of these are practical 'technical' networks – the organisation of raw materials, manufacturing material in anticipation of a task to be undertaken elsewhere. Other relationships include sets of knowledge about the world and its properties: microliths, for example, may have persisted over time because they provided a vehicle for metaphors about the wider obligations of society. Blade working itself may have been considered an appropriate way of treating material with respect. Such accounts stress that craft traditions were learnt, not blindly inherited, but a vital medium of social reproduction, central to the texture of daily life. My accounts of these processes have been heavily biased towards stone, because of conditions of preservation, but equally complex sets of relationships would have surrounded the working of many and varied materials: from bone and antler (48) through to wood and reeds. Indeed, as highlighted in the previous chapter, bone and antler bevel-ended tools can be seen to be a complex outcome of competing demands. Archaeological objects are not simply passive reflections of what happened in the past, but formed part of the ebb and flow of social life in the past and were constitutive of its rich texture.

FURTHER READING

A range of papers touch on the issues covered in the chapter. Although complex, Tim Ingold's 1993 paper introduces the concept of the taskscape, which has proved very influential in hunter-gatherer archaeology in Britain. His 2000 book *Perception of the Environment* is challenging and illuminating: it is also, at times, hard work. Chantal Conneller and Danny Hind's papers give very strong examples of putting these ideas to practice in mesolithic archaeology. Lesley McFadyen offers a powerful discussion of how landscape, taskscape and materiality can be combined to create a new kind of archaeology of place. Alan Saville (2004) and Bill Finlayson (1995) discuss bevel-ended tools. Zvelebil (2003) examines hunter-gatherer world views. A suite of papers by Nyree Finlay help reconsider stone working in mesolithic Britain and Ireland; some examples are drawn from her work as part of the Southern Hebrides Mesolithic Project. Three forthcoming papers, one by Chantal and myself, two by me, discuss stone craft as a form of knowledge and technology more generally. Finally, Taçon and Sillitoe & Hardy give different ethnographic perspectives, see also Hampton in chapter 4.

Conneller, C.J. 2000. 'Fragmented Space? Hunter-gatherer-landscapes of the Vale of Pickering'. *Archaeological Review from Cambridge* 17(1): 139-150

Conneller, C.J. 2001. 'Hunter-gatherers in the landscape: technical economies of the Vale of Pickering' in K.J. Fewster and M. Zvelebil (eds), *Ethnoarchaeology and Hunter-Gatherers: Pictures at an Exhibition*, 1-11.(Oxford: BAR International Series 955)

Finlay, N. 2003. 'Microliths and multiple authorship' in L. Larsson, H. Kindgren, K. Knutsson, D. Loeffler and A. Åkerlund (eds) *Mesolithic on the move: papers presented at the Sixth International Conference on the Mesolithic in Europe, Stockholm 2000, 169-178*. (Oxford: Oxbow)

Finlay, N. 2003. 'Cache and carry: defining moments in the Irish later mesolithic' in L. Bevan and J. Moore (eds) *Peopling the mesolithic in a northern environment*, 87-94. (Oxford: British Archaeological Reports, International series 1157)

Finlay, N. 1997. 'Kid-knapping' in J. Moore and E. Scott (eds) *Invisible people and processes: writing gender and childhood into European archaeology*, 203-212. (London: Leicester University Press)

Finlay, N. 2000. 'Microliths in the making' in R. Young (ed.) *Mesolithic lifeways: current research from Britain and Ireland*, 23-32. (Leicester: Leicester University Monographs)

Finlayson, B. 1995. 'Complexity in the Mesolithic of the Western Scottish Seaboard' in Fischer, A. (ed.) *Man and Sea in the Mesolithic*, 261-4. (Oxford: Oxbow)

Hind, D. 2004a. 'Where many paths meet: towards an integrated theory of landscape and technology' in A.M. Chadwick (ed.) *Stories from the Landscape: Archaeologies of Inhabitation*, 35-51. BAR International Series S1238. (Oxford: Archaeopress)

Ingold, T. 1993. 'The Temporality of Landscape' *World Archaeology* 25(2): 152-174

Ingold, T. 2000. 'The Perception of the environment: essays in livelihood, dwelling and skill' (London: Routledge)

McFadyen, L. forthcoming. 'Landscape' in C. Conneller and G. Warren (eds) *Mesolithic Britain and Ireland: new approaches*. (Stroud: Tempus Publishing)

Mithen, S.J. 2000. 'Hunter-gatherer landscape archaeology: The Southern Hebrides Mesolithic Project 1988-98'. (Cambridge: McDonald Institute Monographs)

Saville, A. 2004. 'The Material Culture of Mesolithic Scotland' in A. Saville (ed.) *Mesolithic Scotland and its Neighbours: the early Holocene prehistory of Scotland its British and Irish context, and some Northern European perspectives*, 185-220. (Edinburgh: Society of Antiquaries of Scotland)

Sillitoe, P. and Hardy, K. 2003. 'Living Lithics. Ethnography in Highland Papua New Guinea' *Antiquity* 297: 555-66

Spuffod, F. 1996. 'I May Be Some Time: Ice and the English Imagination'. (London: Faber & Faber)

Taçon, P. 1991. 'The power of stone: symbolic aspects of stone use and tool development in western Arnhem Land, Australia' in *Antiquity* 65: 192-207

49 Test pit excavation of a mesolithic site at Shiplaw, Eddleston valley, Scottish Borders. © *G. Warren*

Warren, G.M. and Conneller, C. forthcoming. 'Analyses of Mesolithic assemblages from the Sands of Forvie, Aberdeenshire'

Warren, G.M. forthcoming. 'The archaeology of the mesolithic in eastern Scotland: deconstructing culture, constructing identity' in K. Pedersen and C. Waddington (eds) *The Late Palaeolithic and Mesolithic of the North Sea Basin and Littoral*

Warren, G.M. forthcoming. 'Technology' in C. Conneller and G.M Warren (eds) *Mesolithic Britain and Ireland: new approaches*. (Stroud: Tempus Publishing)

Zvelebil, M. 2003. 'People behind the lithics. Social life and social conditions of Mesolithic communities in Temperate Europe' in L. Bevan and J. Moore (eds) *Peopling the mesolithic in a northern environment*, 1-26. (Oxford: BAR international series 1157)

AN INTERJECTION

All of this talk of craft and skill is fine, but what about the skills of mesolithic archaeology! How can I get involved in the practical side of mesolithic archaeology? How, for example, are all of these archaeological sites found?

There are lots of ways of getting involved in mesolithic archaeology, and many of them relate closely to the process of discovery. Put crudely, archaeology in Scotland involves three related approaches. Firstly, university or museum archaeologists organise research excavations or related projects, sometimes working in particular areas for long periods of time. The Southern Hebrides Mesolithic Project, which I have often referenced, is a good example of this. Secondly, archaeology forms part of the development process in Scotland, and works on a polluter pays principle: if you want to build a supermarket or road, for example, as part of the planning process you are required to assess the archaeological impact of this, and possibly to pay for any archaeology threatened by the development. Sites such as Fife Ness were discovered in this way.

In the case of mesolithic archaeology there is an important third way of being involved. Because lots of mesolithic archaeology relies on stone tools, one of the most useful things is understanding the distribution of them across the landscape. Interested members of the public have collected stone tools for a long time in Scotland, and when these people collaborate with archaeological institutions the benefits to archaeological knowledge are immense. Many of the sites I've been talking about in the Upper Tweed Valley, for example, were discovered by Bob Knox, whose sharp eyes spotted stone tools eroding from footpaths and in fields in and around his home. Bob then became involved in his local archaeological society – the Peebles Archaeological Society – and as an organisation, they are now involved in more formal fieldwalking and test-pitting programmes (49), systematically examining areas of the landscape for artefacts and providing very important information on the distribution of early prehistoric activity. The value of this work was conditional on two things: Bob kept very good records of the exact locations of his finds, and he collaborated with the appropriate institutions. To collect artefacts without any record of where they are from, or to collect them without telling anyone, destroys the archaeological record. There are legal requirements and protections surrounding archaeological materials, and anything that someone discovers must be reported to a museum.

So how could I get involved?

It depends on where you are, and what you want to do. You could try and get in touch with your local archaeological society, young archaeologists club, or volunteer to assist on a research dig. You can find out information about these through the Council for Scottish Archaeology, a charity with regular newsletters and information updates (http://www.scottisharchaeology.org.uk/). At a British level, the Council for British Archaeology has similar links and roles (http://www.britarch.ac.uk/). Some very important projects rely hugely on assistance from members of the public: Shorewatch, for example, (http://www.shorewatch.co.uk/) carries out vital work examining the coasts of Scotland for archaeological features.

Although lots of people can make a contribution to mesolithic (and other) archaeology, it is vital that people don't start just wandering off and collecting artefacts. By all means keep your eyes peeled, but make sure you inform the relevant archaeological bodies if you do think you've found anything. Most importantly, work within an existing archaeology group if possible – it'll probably be more fun to work with people than on your own, and it will help you learn more about the material that you are trying to find.

6

SPACE AND PLACE

I argued in the last chapters that tasks formed part of networks creating links between the 'sites' that archaeologists spend so much time discussing. Of course, it is clear that in order to understand mobile communities one cannot just discuss single sites, but must consider the wider landscapes in which people lived (50). So far my accounts of these landscapes have been thin: I have not outlined, in detail, the contexts within which people's actions took place; the kinds of places and spaces that characterised the mesolithic world in Scotland. Of course the nature of these places and social relations was, to a large degree, created by routines of skilled labour: spaces devoted to basketry, or where people learnt the skills of watching game, developed their character as places through the tasks carried out within them. And the physical characteristics of varied places within the mesolithic landscape also created particular possibilities for understanding the world: the ways in which a path facilitated movement, or the number of people that could shelter in a building.

Place might be understood as a particular part of space, an aspect of the world picked up on by human attention – and demarcated from other spaces, possibly by being named, or through other forms of people's action. Thus, the study of place incorporates the study of ancient architecture – and architecture is, in a basic sense, a way of structuring the experience of space and place, and of course, time. However, places were also created by acts of naming or other forms of inhabitation not characterised by building: paths, clearings, mountains, rivers and trees. Many of these were not altered by human activity at all, and some were altered in only minor ways – an offering laid at the foot of a rock, a carving on an old tree. In other examples, there is a clear link between forms of architecture and the location. At Morton, Fife, a series of light structures was erected over time on a low island of volcanic rock, rising above a swamp. Reconstructions of these structures are vague, but they appear to have included small wind breaks set around hearths, sometimes in scoops. Sleeping areas have also been identified and there is evidence of stone working taking place around the fire. One occupation appears to have made use of, perhaps even quarried, the volcanic rock of the outcrop in order to provide part of the structure. This is a fine illustration of the ways in which architecture picks up upon, and modifies the 'natural' characteristics of place.

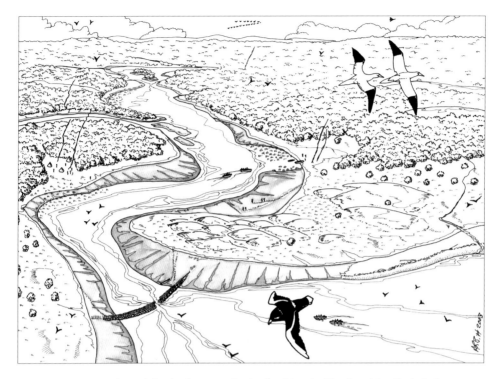

50 Reconstruction of mesolithic landscape at the Sands of Forvie, Aberdeenshire. © *A. Braby*

In the modern world, with such a strong distinction between the natural and cultural, we are sometimes too rigid, thinking of places as humanly constructed architectural features against a natural background. A range of hunter-gatherer ethnography, some of which was reviewed in chapter 3, suggests that a strong distinction between constructed spaces and a natural background would be inappropriate. In this chapter I therefore address understandings of both the landscape and architecture, seeing them as strongly interlinked.

HUNTER–GATHERER LANDSCAPES

Recent years have seen increased attention paid to the ways in which contemporary or near contemporary hunter-gatherers in the northern temperate forests of Eurasia, especially Siberia, understand their landscapes. Put simply, these landscapes are redolent with meaning being generated by the activities of spirits, animals and other agencies.

The basic model, with much local variation, is that northern hunter-gatherers today live in a three-tiered universe of upper-world (sky), middle-world (earth) and lower-/underworld (underground) with movement of spirits between these levels. This cosmological understanding is also grounded in features of the landscape: thus the underworld is both below and to the north, i.e. the cold, which is also the direction that the main rivers in Siberia flow, and downstream movement is associated with the underworld. All beings (including things we in the modern West would classify as both animate and inanimate) have spirits, and relationships with controlling spirits are often based around varied models of reciprocity, i.e. you give in order to receive. Particular individuals may have great powers in communicating with spirits, often involving trance and 'spirit journeys' – these are shamans. Particular places in the landscape are understood to facilitate communication between the spirit levels: for example, rivers serve as an important axis for movement between the differing worlds, and rapids and waterfalls are considered especially significant in this regard. Certain animals are also associated with the ability to communicate between different levels, especially water birds. Bears are very important in such world-views and were sometimes held in captivity, or semi-tamed in order to be sacrificed at the appropriate times.

Peter Jordan has made an especially significant contribution to these debates, stressing that this meaningful landscape is actively created by hunter-gatherers through particular forms of behaviour that have archaeological correlates. Jordan undertook anthropo-logical fieldwork with the Eastern Khanty of boreal western Siberia, and, amongst other things, focused on how material practices related to, and helped maintain, wider bodies of knowledge. For example, the understanding that movement downstream on a river is associated with the underworld is maintained by the practice that a village (or *yurt*) will always locate its cemetery downstream or inland, in order to avoid the spiritual pollution from the dead that might result if it was located upstream. When a new building is added to a *yurt* it is always located upstream, even to the extent that rebuilding a house *in situ* would involve a symbolic shift of a few metres upstream.

Another example comes from the deposition of animal bones, and especially those of the elk. Elk, as with all other animals, have spirits and are controlled by the spirit masters. The process of hunting is understood within the broad framework of reciprocity: 'the elk is thought to give itself up to the hunter as an act of personal choice ... in return for appropriate treatment of the carcass and the bones on the part of the hunter'. (Jordan, P. 2001 'Ideology, Material Culture and Khanty ritual landscapes in western Siberia' in K.J. Fewster and M. Zvelebil (eds) *Ethnoarcheology and Hunter-Gatherers: Pictures at an Exhibition*. BAR International Series 955, p.29). The correct treatment of material is vital to the circulation of the spirits. Thus the heart and head of the elk, where its soul resides, is deposited in a special location in the forest, where they are safe from being chewed by dogs, which would be considered a very poor treatment of the bones. Archaeologically speaking, what results are discrete deposits of elk bones, sometimes with an emphasis on particular parts of the skeleton that may be interpreted as middens.

This northern world-view has become a popular way of interpreting the mesolithic in Europe. Marek Zvelebil has argued that many features of the mesolithic make sense when considered in this way. For example, rock carvings at Nämforsen, Sweden, are located at the last rapids on the River Angerman and include many shamanic images and associations. Zvelebil suggests that the Nämforsen carvings are located at the entrance to the underworld (the last rapids before the sea), and that many of the images relate to the circulation of souls of elk in such world-views. Some mesolithic burials are associated with water birds, and especially swans. As noted above, such birds were understood as facilitating communication and transport between the spirit worlds: in one striking example from Vedbaek, Denmark, a young woman and a newborn child are buried together, with the child laid on a swan's wing. The presence of the swan's wing may have been considered a way of assisting the child in moving between the spirit worlds; and the act of including it in the grave must have helped the mourners cope with such a tragedy. Finally, and at a slightly greater geographical remove, a brown bear with evidence of a thong tied around its jaw, assumedly in order to keep it captive or tame, has been discovered in the late mesolithic of the French Alps at La Grande-Rivoire, Isère. Based on deformation of the lower jaw the bone specialists argue that the thong was tied at between four and seven months and the bear died at six years old. Keeping an animal tamed for this length of time was likely to have been associated with shamanic world-views.

These accounts have greatly enriched understandings of the mesolithic landscape in north-west Europe. However, their impact on the Scottish mesolithic is less clear. Put simply, there is little evidence that clearly fits into this kind of picture: not least because of preservation biases and research traditions. Looking more broadly at Britain and Ireland in the mesolithic, Richard Chatterton has argued that careful deposition of animal remains into watery contexts, sometimes weighed down with trees or rocks, and the structured deposition of stone tools into rivers were both common. But none of Richard's examples come from Scotland. This presents a common archaeological problem: is the absence of the evidence from Scotland simply a product of the generally poor preservation of material in this region, or does this suggest that the mesolithic inhabitants of this region held different world-views? The answer is probably a little of both, and this forces the identification of new ways of considering the data.

Stone axes were frequently deposited in rivers in Ireland and the south of England during the mesolithic, and it is possible that these tools held important symbolic associations that made their deposition in this way appropriate. Unfortunately, one of the characteristic features of the lithic industries of mesolithic Scotland is the absence of chipped or polished axes found in the rest of Britain and Ireland. Only one possible

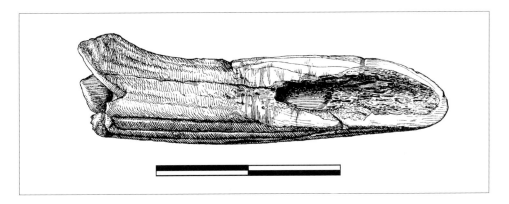

51 Antler mattock from Risga. Scale in 5cm divisions. Reproduced at 1:2. *After Lacaille 1954 Fig 103*

52 Landscape at Oliclett, Caithness. © M. Pannett

mesolithic axe head, from Cambwell, near Biggar, has been identified. The absence of axes from Scotland is generally believed to reflect the generally small size of the raw materials available. However, antler mattocks are a relatively common find on mesolithic sites with suitable preservation, and experiments have demonstrated that antler operates effectively as an axe. It seems possible that antler mattocks functioned as axes in Scotland. This suggests that examining the contexts of discovery of these mattocks might be useful. Most of the finds of organic tools from Scotland come from either middens or riverine/estuarine contexts. Again, it is difficult to assess the significance of these objects: the riverine bias may simply indicate the existence of preserving contexts rather than any deliberate choice to deposit material into rivers. Similarly the presence of artefacts on middens is again affected by preservation biases.

The presence of organic tools in association with the skeletons of whales found in the carse clays of the Forth is of more interest. At Meiklewood, the famous antler beam mattock (22) was recovered 'resting upon the front of the skull and lying vertically in the blue silt'. In other examples the associations were less close; at Airthrey Castle and Causewayhead antler tools were 'close to' the skeletons, although the role of the tides in shifting artefacts should be noted in these cases. At both Meiklewood and Burnbank the tools were hafted: although poorly understood the Burnbank example seems likely to have been another mattock. Given the length of time involved in manufacturing and hafting antler tools, the chance loss of such artefacts seems unlikely. And, given the significance of axes in the mesolithic of the British Isles, discussed above, the finding of a hafted axe deposited on the skull of a whale is hard to reconcile with chance loss. It is therefore possible that these associations were created through deliberate acts of deposition. Whales were the largest animal encountered by mesolithic communities in Scotland, and their appearance through strandings, or taking by the hunt, must have been a very significant event, not least if such events provided a context for a communal gathering to consume large quantities of food. That whales are creatures of the sea that breathe air may also have been significant. Thinking in terms of the northern cosmology outlined above, such animals might have been perceived as messengers between spirit realms. Certainly their stranding might have been perceived in an analogous way to animal offering themselves to the hunters.

Fragments of antler beam mattocks are also common in middens from western Scotland (51). Often interpreted as fragments from use or ready for recycling, it is worth considering the reasons for the deposition of material on these middens. The reasons for the formation of midden deposits are not clear, but a stress on fragmentation does seem to be significant, with fragments of human and animal bodies present (see chapter 7). Thinking again about their possible use as axes, and symbolic associations with this, the deposition of fragments in this context may have been more meaningful than often supposed.

The evidence from the artefacts associated with whales thus provides some possible indication of how the deposition of material culture may have been tied into broader schemes of meaning. It would be tempting to import more details from the northern hunter-gatherer analogy, and talk of rivers and rapids as meeting places of spirit worlds, of upstream and downstream and of sacred hills. But the evidence does not allow this. Such analogies have become very common in recent mesolithic archaeology, and there is a danger of losing some of the specific character of the archaeological record in different regions.

AN OLD LAND

The clearest evidence in Scotland for how people understood their landscape comes from the repeated use of 'old' locations for differing activities. One of the most striking examples of this is seen at Morton, Fife. As noted earlier, Morton was a low volcanic island above reed swamp, although its setting has been greatly affected by changing sea levels. Clive Bonsall has argued that the complex history of occupation at Morton is intimately associated with these changing sea levels. He suggests that the site was occupied during a period of high sea level in the early mesolithic, probably in and around the mid-ninth millennium BC, and the abandoned until sea levels again rose close to the site, some time after the mid-sixth millennium BC. Radiocarbon dates from the site are unreliable, but indicate some activity throughout the fifth millennium, and possibly earlier. Morton then demonstrates a hunter-gatherer reoccupation of a site used some 3000 years earlier. Some archaeologists argue that this is a deliberate referencing of the past, and a way of making connections. In the case of Morton, this argument is difficult to assess. Morton was an important island above marshes, a prime location for hunter-gatherers. The resettlement may simply be coincidence. But, even if it was, the coincidence must have led to the discovery of old stone tools on the site, including microliths unlike those made by the occupants. Stories would have been told of these artefacts, and of the activities of the ancestors who had made the world.

Melli Pannett has recently argued that the site of Oliclett, Caithness, offered visual reminders of previous generations of activity to those who sat and worked stone there, in the form of older scatters of stone (52). This is a very interesting idea as, on some sites, the sheer density of material made these reminders of previous lives very visible. The best interpretation of activity on the Sands of Forvie, for example, is probably repeated small visits, with stone-tool production being tied into a wider suite of activities, including processing of large amounts of vegetable matter. These repeated occupations, sometimes around fireplaces, shifted across a ridge that was slowly being covered by sand. Wherever people looked, flint would have been visible, slowly eroding out of or being buried by the ceaseless actions of the sands (*colour plate 17*). These flints offered continual prompts of the correctness of people's actions – and at Forvie, one of the striking features of the assemblage is how little evidence there is of people reusing this older material, despite the fact that much of it was of a high enough quality to work. It seems almost as if people chose to leave the material in the ground.

In the west, many mesolithic sites indicate long-term use: radiocarbon dates from Rùm, for example, cover a period of a thousand years, although the actual period(s) of occupation may have been shorter. Recent work in the Southern Hebrides has also identified the importance of 'persistent places'; Steve Mithen notes that sites such as Bolsay Farm, Kindrochid and Rockside on Islay:

> had presumably been originally selected for occupation on ecological grounds by weighing up various costs and benefits of this locality over others. But people are equally likely to have re-visited the site without again making such calculations: the landscape rapidly became one with a history and that history made a substantial influence on human movement and settlement...
>
> Mithen, S. 2000 *Hunter-gatherer landscape archaeology: The Southern Hebrides Mesolithic Project 1988-98*. McDonald Institute Monographs, Oxbow books, Oxford p. 606

The sense that the Scottish landscape was an old one in the mesolithic is strong. Arguably, certain places carried powerful associations with time depth. It is important to be clear here: the emphasis on previous activity need not have been considered a link with the distant past: many hunter-gatherers conceptualise of time as circular. For example, in Siberia, mammoth remains preserved in permafrost are considered part of the present, but as originating from the underworld. In a similar way, the sense of return evoked on many mesolithic sites in Scotland may not be an indication of a sense of deep time: rather the objects encountered on these visits may have been considered an active part of the present, possibly evidence of the active role of the spirits in the landscape, and therefore of the need to manage your relationship with these beings. Nowhere is this sense clearer than on middens.

The role of middens within the mesolithic landscape has seen much attention in recent years (*colour plate 18*). Shell middens have shifted from being discussed simply in terms of their nutritional content, to being considered as monuments of the mesolithic, deliberate constructions that tied communities to places. Mesolithic middens, however, are a little more slippery than some models suggest. Many are much less monumental than recent debates allow, hidden in caves, or tucked away behind rock outcrops. Furthermore, the funerary associations that have inspired many of the recent discussions are less common than once supposed. Nevertheless, some middens appear to have resulted from long-

Above: 53 Reconstructed mesolithic building at Archaeolink, Aberdeenshire.
© *G. Warren*

Right: 54 Sub-surface features at Rùm.
Wickham-Jones 1990 Ill 96

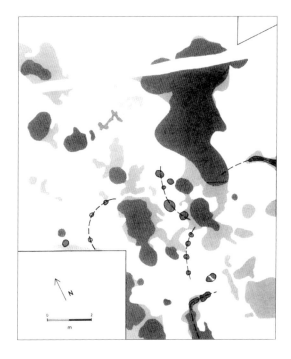

term patterns of activity: the Oronsay middens accumulated over varied lengths of time, but often many hundreds of years. These time periods are replicated on other middens; for example, radiocarbon dates from Morton B span approximately a thousand years. This pattern requires explanation.

Middens are interesting as architecture, and provide a useful link to the more explicit discussion of 'built' places in the following section. Middens do not accumulate by accident, but result from the repetition of a single action, the decision to dispose

55 Reconstruction drawings based on the remains at Rúm. *Wickham-Jones 1990 Ill 98; © A. Braby*

of particular kinds of materials in particular places. Sometimes, these repeated acts took place over the long term. Archaeologists have seldom asked why this stability in attitudes to materiality existed: there is no obvious reason that one should always throw food remains away in the same places. Thinking back to the discussion of the Siberian Khanty it is also clear that deposits of animal bones often embody complex meanings.

Strikingly, the surfaces of middens themselves appear to have been utilised for other activities: arcs of stone and levelled areas were identified at Morton B and Paul Mellars excavated evidence for hearths and other features within the Oronsay middens. On the face of it, this is an unusual decision: choosing to sit on top of an uncomfortable mound of presumably smelly waste material. Along with the sense that the repeated deposition of material itself deserves explanation, the presence of these activity areas also raises questions. This indicates a stress on the processes by which middens come into being: that it was important to act in certain kinds of ways on these sites. In this regard it may be relevant to think of at least some mesolithic middens as visible histories of actions: as a place in the landscape where people could associate their acts with those of previous generations, or with the activities of those now transformed into spirits. The middens provided a sense of ontological security; a sense that this was the appropriate way of acting. These were places where it was appropriate to carry out certain acts and one's identity was reiterated by acting in these ways.

THE BUILT ENVIRONMENT

The topic of mesolithic architecture in Scotland has, until recently, received little discussion. The remains of most buildings were fragmentary, and often archaeologists were left trying to link up scattered post-holes and pits in order to make coherent results. Commonly, the reconstruction of these buildings was of tent-like structures, drawing heavily on ethnographic analogies (53). The interpretation of the remains from Rùm offers a good illustration (54 and 55). Here Caroline Wickham-Jones interpreted a complex of scoops, posts and pits as demonstrating arcs of related stake-holes that once supported structures. Even after the arcs were identified, however, the nature of the structures they represented remained unclear, and reconstruction drawings from the site include alternative possibilities: closed tents or open wind breaks. The difficulties of interpreting how these structures influenced people's lives are exacerbated because of the lack of contextual details associated with them: a scatter of stone or other materials, often itself a complex palimpsest of different activities.

Recent changes have helped invigorate the study of mesolithic buildings, including the general reawakening of interest in social relations in the mesolithic period. A recent paper by Caroline Wickham-Jones offers a detailed review of mesolithic architecture in Scotland, concluding that 'when I set out to write this paper I had no idea of the wealth of structural evidence that existed from Scottish mesolithic sites, not of the richness and variety': the paper is a significant step in changing understandings of architecture in the period. More dramatically, recent discoveries challenge perceptions of mesolithic architecture; most notably, excavations at East Barns, near Dunbar, as well as Howick, in Northumberland, and most recently at Lesmurdie Road, Elgin, have revealed evidence of substantial post-defined mesolithic buildings (discussed in more detail below). These in turn have refocused attention on older sites, with increased confidence in the possibilities of mesolithic architecture. As noted above, however, these buildings should not be separated from the social relations that constituted place, and in particular from the networks of tasks and activities that provided the texture and rhythms of daily lives. Constituted by tasks, and in turn part of the fabric of life, mesolithic buildings require more attention than they have often received. In my exploration of architectural places here I start at the smallest scale, and work up.

BURNING QUESTIONS

One of the more evocative mesolithic sites in Scotland lies on the shores of the Solway Firth. At Redkirk Point, Gretna, a pear-shaped hollow about 1 x 0.6m and 25cm deep was filled with burnt sands, charcoal, and towards the base was a semi-circular setting of burnt sandstone interpreted as a hearth. The site dates to some time in the centuries either side of 7000 BC, and was sealed by deposits of the maximum marine transgression in the region. No artefacts were recovered from Redkirk and no further structural evidence was identified. Coastal defences now bury the site.

To my mind Redkirk is resonant because it is one of the simplest forms of architecturally modified place – a built fireplace and the consequent transformation of space around it. Possibly here a low scoop was used to place the fire, protecting it slightly from the wind. This place, located above a low and marshy foreshore was then a focus for activity for a short time period. Often, archaeologists study the deposition of artefacts in order to identify patterns of activity. In the mesolithic in Scotland, this is especially dependent on the deposition of stone tools. It is sometimes easy to forget that many places and routines may not have involved stone tools. Once again, we are reminded that the Stone Age only appears to be dominated by stone. Redkirk, because of the difficulty in interpreting the site, is also evocative of the place of fires in people's lives. Redkirk may have been a fire around which stories were told, or over which a snack was cooked, or to warm the participants of a funerary ceremony: of course, all three of these possibilities could have been combined in the same event. Whichever, and it is certain that the details elude us, the scale of the hollow suggests an intimacy to the place – a small group, or an individual, once rested here: perhaps for an hour, perhaps a day. As anyone who has sat around a fire knows, the presence of the flame provides a structure to space, influenced by the wind, the direction of smoke blow, and the heat and light provided by the fire. That these are transient features is a further reminder of the challenge of thinking about mesolithic places. The fire results from a sequence of acts: it takes time to build; to collect stone for the hearth and gather fuel from surrounding areas; to prepare tinder and generate a flame. The need for firewood of differing kinds creates significant demands on people's time and, indeed, the exhaustion of firewood in a particular locale may have prompted a decision to move on to another spot. These demands must have been balanced with other tasks, perhaps especially the preparation of food. Perhaps this highlights the social focus of the fire, as well as its practical benefits. In a general sense the fire provided warmth and light for tricky tasks, such as retooling: striking blades and snapping them to the appropriate lengths, melting resins and fixing new teeth in fishing spears. Of course, many of these were routine activities, carried out with little thought, and whilst engaged in conversation and gossip. At Forvie, there are hints of areas next to the fire where cores were worked, along with scraping and other activities carried out a little further from its warmth.

Although it is seldom commented upon, fireplaces are an important feature of the archaeological record of the mesolithic period, and it seems that they frequently provided an important focus for varied activity. Of course, there are problems here – in an archaeological sense fire is a preserver of materials through charring, and fire and associated activities are archaeologically quite visible. It is important not to confuse the archaeological visibility of a phenomenon with its ancient significance. Nevertheless, across Scotland hints of small scatters of worked stone in association with fires are strong: small concentrations of material with evidence of burning are found at varied sites under the modern centre of Aberdeen, and at the Sands of Forvie. Many fireplaces seem to have formed part of larger structures, or to have been repeatedly set in the same places. At Morton for example, fires are sometimes associated with small windbreaks, a pattern also seen at Fife Ness. Here a small arc of pits surrounds a central hearth with a larger pit across the hearth from the structure. At Barsalloch, in Dumfries and Galloway, fireplaces were found in a natural sandy hollow – sometimes placed within pits in this hollow. Stone settings found on the site may indicate some shelters – although these are difficult to interpret.

Based on observations of living hunter-gatherers, some archaeologists, such as Lewis Binford, have developed models of how the space around fireplaces accumulates debris – with a 'toss and drop zone' describing characteristic distributions of rubbish. Immediately around people's seats small rubbish builds up, whilst larger pieces are thrown over, or through the fire. These models are interesting, but sometimes risk turning fireplaces into rather mechanical places. Fires were not places of either work or leisure – these distinctions may have held little meaning in prehistory. Fires helped to provide contexts within which people interacted, and, as stated above, often the sense is of some intimacy in the ways in which small groups used these spaces. Thinking of the fire as a source of light and heat, and as the focal point for a group, becomes even more significant when considering the long winter nights characteristic of northern Scotland. At these times the social world may have revolved around the pockets of light provided by fires and many of the routine tasks people undertook were associated with feeding and tending the fire. Fire itself is likely to have been an especially significant symbolic referent. Fire played a major role in transformations of many kinds: from raw to cooked food, for instance, as well as in the manufacture of resins of differing kinds. The control of fire marked humans out from all other animals, with the possible exception of the spirits responsible for lightning. Penny Spikins has carried out ethnographic research amongst the Selk'nam, hunter-gatherers of the Tierra del Fuego in South America, and argues that fire serves as a way of alerting others to danger, advertising one's presence in order to ask permission to enter a territory, or as other ways of communicating.

In fact, some sites indicate rather more complexity to people's relationships with fire and with the deposition of rubbish. At Newton, Islay, for example, numerous fires were placed in a sub-rectangular or circular building with a pitched roof and sunken floor, most likely at some time between c.7050-6450 BC. The excavators note the presence of deposits of midden material in the structure, but argue that 'it is difficult to imagine how such deposits accumulated within an active inhabitation'. They suggest that midden deposits were placed within the structure intermittently, with occupation including fires taking place on these surfaces. The parallels here with the discussion of shell middens are striking, with an emphasis on how people actively chose to deposit midden material, and then occupy these surfaces. Again, it is interesting to note the ways that materials from different locations are brought together in the definition of a place: waste material, fuel for the fire, and people with all of their attendant materials. Similar patterns can also be identified at Rùm, where a natural hollow was used as a working area, then deliberately infilled with midden material including organics and lithics. A hollow and two pits were then cut into this feature and two distinctive steep pits with posts placed in the bottom: the excavator noted the possibility that the posts acted as markers for the pits. These pits were also deliberately backfilled. In this context, the enigmatic deposit of hazelnuts into a hollow, possibly a sunken floor of a house, at Staosnaig should be noted. Richard Chatterton has argued that such deposits of midden material may have been associated with ideas of renewal and regeneration. These discussions suggest that some understandings of what mesolithic Scottish architecture indicates require rethinking. Deposits of material, pits and fireplaces may all have held much more social significance than is commonly supposed. Certainly this reminds us that in the past as well as today, buildings have complex associations, and should not just be interpreted simply as domestic structures where mundane tasks were carried out. Just as in the discussions of artefacts, from the possibilities of symbolic associations through to the network of tasks involved in the creation of place, and then undertaken there, an understanding of mesolithic places as microcosms of wider landscapes becomes possible.

The debate about the best interpretation of mesolithic architecture been highlighted by the recent discovery of significant numbers of large substantial post-defined buildings, mentioned briefly above. These wonderful structures have, rightly, been the focus of much discussion. Unfortunately, few of the newly discovered sites are published in detail at this stage, which places limits on discussion.

The site at Howick is now located on the Northumberland coast, and was discovered through the presence of lithics in an eroding cliff section. The site, which was occupied c.7800 BC, was probably a hundred metres or so back from the sea in the mesolithic. The building is truncated by erosion to the east, but comprised a circular sunken area with an interior ring of posts (about 10-15cm thick). The building contained a series of intercutting central hearths and contained deep deposits of debris including 16,000 lithics. The building itself was rebuilt at least twice. Interestingly, despite occasional finds of marine molluscs, there is little evidence of extensive use of marine resources, although burnt bones of wild pig, fox, birds and a dog or wolf were identified along with large numbers of hazelnuts. Excavations in the surrounding area revealed no further mesolithic features although mesolithic flint working is common along this coastline.

There are striking similarities between Howick and a mesolithic building of similar age identified at Mount Sandel in Northern Ireland. At Mount Sandel a low scoop was the focus for a circular building some 6m in diameter, constructed out of small stakes and posts. The excavator, Peter Woodman, noted the possibility that turf was banked up to provide one side of the building. The building been reconstructed on the same spot at least four times. Again, a series of inter-cutting central hearths were identified, and as at Howick a mass of stone working and other debris was found. The building was found in the centre of a mass of pits and other features.

Recent excavations at East Barns, near Dunbar, have revealed a similar structure, also dating to c.7800 BC and measuring 6.8 x 6.2m. Here a large natural hollow had its edges modified, and a ring of post-holes (20-25cm thick) placed just inside this; some angled towards the centre of the building, some vertical. The excavator, John Gooder of AOC archaeology, interprets the building as having a timber framework supporting a domed or pitched roof. A number of pits and other features inside the building are noted, as well as scatters of lithics and other features outside.

Whilst there are differences in the detail of these buildings they demonstrate the existence of a widespread architectural tradition in the centuries following 8000 BC. Substantial in construction, and modifying natural hollows or creating their own, much of the excitement of these new finds lies in the challenges they pose to dominant models. Most archaeologists have supposed that mobility formed a key part of people's lives, and the light character of most excavated structures bore witness to this. The existence of substantial buildings, often located in areas with access to a variety of resources is a challenge to such notions, and analyses of the faunal and other remains from Howick and East Barns have much to contribute. In this regard it is notable that analyses of Mountt Sandel established that occupation at the site could have lasted for much of the year. Most interpretations have suggested that such buildings could have comfortably housed five to six people, and images of the nuclear family are hard to escape: even if such images are likely to be misleading, not least because modern conception of the nuclear family may not be appropriate for all times and places.

These new buildings have also sparked off debate about what kind of role they played in the mesolithic landscape. Simplifying crudely, this can be characterised as an opposition between seeing the structures as houses or homes, and interpreting them as some kind of ritual building. Based on an ethnographic study of hunter gatherers in Tierra del Fuego, Penny Spikins highlighted the importance of the fact that: 'for all that the economic, social and religious life of the Selk'nam was very complex, very little remains in the archaeological record.' (Spikins, P. 2003 *Prehistoric People of the Pennines: reconstructing the lifestyles of Mesolithic hunter-gatherers on Marsden Moor*. West Yorkshire Archaeology Service, p.71). Often, simply stone tools and fireplaces would remain, with very rare examples of structural evidence. Most of the time the Selk'nam lived in very light tents and other shelters, which would be unlikely to leave much archaeological trace. The only exception would be the sacred tent, or *choza*, erected during an important ceremony called the Hain. The *choza* was built to a specific, and repeated structure, which connected the location of posts to the skies. Penny argues that the *choza* would probably be misinterpreted as a routine dwelling, rather than as a specialist ritual structure.

The point is not whether any of these new structures are houses or ritual centres. To frame the question in this way falls into a classic dualism: ritual versus mundane, sacred versus profane. Enough ethnography has already been adduced in this book to show that hunter-gatherers are very unlikely to have conceived of the world in this way. In any case, we don't behave in this way today: our houses are structured around a series of complex relationships between people and things and different bodies of meaning. Houses may contain religious icons, or family heirlooms, set in certain locations to overlook particular activities as reminders of presences. Houses contain public and private spaces, spaces where it is appropriate to behave in particular ways. It was likely the same in the mesolithic. At Mount Sandel, for example, analysis of the distribution of lithics identified particular places around the structure where different activities were carried out.

Rather than think of the buildings as houses or ritual places it is probably more useful to pay more critical attention to the details of their construction and use; and here the full publication of the structures is awaited eagerly. Even at this stage, however, certain patterns in the evidence are of interest, and suggest links with themes discussed above. The repeated rebuilding of structures on the same site, for example, may have a practical basis in the presence of a slight scoop – but it may be helpful to think of deliberate rebuildings, or recuttings of hearths in more-or-less the same location as ways of establishing links across time, of making connections with previous occupations of a site. Furthermore the repeated accumulations of debris within these structures, which, following the evidence of Newton, may have been deliberately deposited from elsewhere, is hard to interpret in a practical light.

The construction of these structures involved the building or modification of a scoop and the gathering and preparation of suitable posts, stakes and coverings. At least in the initial stages of use most likely this involved co-operative labour, and the organisation of different tasks: some to collect timber, some to prepare food, others to gather firewood. Other tasks had been carried out long before: preparation of hides for covers, procurement of flint and antler to enable the woodworking required in such constructions. The building itself was the outcome of a complex intermeshing of such obligations. In this sense, to present the buildings as isolated self-contained family homes is fundamentally misleading. Structures such as this expressed community: in terms of wide notions of the 'right' way of building something, through to the mobilisation of the labour and resources needed to actually build it.

REVIEW

This chapter has focused on the character of different spaces and places in the mesolithic landscape, from broad conceptions of sacred places though examinations of different kinds of place. Research on these issues in British and Irish archaeology is in its infancy, and often such concerns have been dismissed. Unfortunately, all too often, the archaeological reluctance to discuss such themes has been because of the questions considered appropriate to ask, and not because of the character of the evidence, which is much richer than has often been supposed. Here I have attempted to sketch some of the key themes in the Scottish evidence. Looking at the spiritual side of things I have highlighted hints of votive deposits suggesting ways in which hunter-gatherers came to terms with certain animals, and suggested that returns to places with evidence of other occupations may have been significant. More mundanely, but strangely silent from our accounts, the role of fire in structuring many routine activities has been stressed, and I have highlighted the possible significance of the production and re-deposition of midden materials of varying kinds. All of these debates highlight the complex interplay between the 'symbolic' and the 'practical' in the generation of the materials studied in mesolithic archaeology. Such debates are thrown into sharp relief by the new structures, and the crude dichotomy between the domestic or the ritual interpretation: more helpful approaches stress the ways in which the creation of these places created certain possibilities for social relations. Spaces and places, constructed within particular understandings of the world, brought people together, and created and sustained differences between them. It is to these communities that the discussion now turns.

FURTHER READING

Arguments about landscape and the ways in which people understand it have become very common in mesolithic archaeology recently. For examples, and a flavour of recent debates, see for example, edited books by Bevan and Moore and Conneller and Warren. Peter Jordan's excellent work is presented in detail in his book *Material Culture and Sacred Landscape* (2003) as well as a number of shorter papers, including in the Bevan and Moore volume. Marek Zvelebil's discussion of world-views is in the same publication. Chatterton's review of ritual has been referred to many times, Milner's discussion of subsistence in the same volume includes arguments about midden formation and analysis. Joshua Pollard's paper (2000) argues for an ancestral aspect to mesolithic landscapes, and Meli Pannett's discussion of Oliclett (forthcoming) offers another way of considering similar themes. Caroline Wickham-Jones's excellent structural review (2004) was published just before all the new houses were found (Waddington et al. 2003, Gooder 2003) and the Mount Sandel example is discussed in Woodman (1985) and Murphy (1996). Binford's *In Pursuit of the Past* is a classic, although taking a rather different tack from that adopted here. Spikins' discussion of the Selk'nam forms part of her book on the Pennines.

Bevan, L. and Moore, J. (ed.) 2003. *Peopling the mesolithic in a northern environment.* (BAR International Series 1157)

Binford, L. 1983. *In Pursuit of the Past: decoding the archaeological record.* (University of California Press)

Chatterton, R. forthcoming. 'Ritual' in C. Conneller and G. Warren (eds) *Mesolithic Britain and Ireland: new approaches.* (Stroud: Tempus Publishing)

Conneller, C. and Warren, G.M. (eds) forthcoming. *Mesolithic Britain and Ireland: new approaches.* (Stroud: Tempus Publishing)

Gooder, J. 2003. 'Excavating the Oldest House in Scotland: East Barns, Dunbar, East Lothian' *Scottish Archaeological News* 42: 1-2

Jordan, P. 2003. *Material Culture and Sacred Landscape: the anthropology of the Siberian Khanty.* (Oxford: Alta Mira Press)

Milner, N. forthcoming. 'Subsistence' in C. Conneller and G. Warren (eds) *Mesolithic Britain and Ireland: new approaches.* (Stroud: Tempus Publishing)

Murphy, E.M. 1996. 'Possible Gender Divisions at the Mesolithic Site of Mount Sandel, Co. Londonderry, Northern Ireland' in *Kvinner Arkeologi Norge* 21: 103–124

Pannett, A. forthcoming. 'A post-processual flight of fancy? Microlith production and the enculturation of landscape in Mesolithic of Caithness' in K.L.R. Pedersen and C. Waddington (eds) *The Late Palaeolithic and Mesolithic of the North Sea Littoral: recent research and emerging issues*. (Oxford: Oxbow)

Pollard, J. 2000. 'Ancestral places in the Mesolithic landscape' in C. Conneller (ed.) 'New approaches to the Paleolithic and Mesolithic'. *Archaeological review from Cambridge* 17: 123–137

Spikins, P. 2002. *Prehistoric People of the Pennines: reconstructing the lifestyles of Mesolithic hunter-gatherers on Marsden Moor*. West Yorkshire Archaeology Service

Waddington, C., Bailey, G., Boomer, I., Milner, N., Pederson, K., Shiel, R. and Stevenson, T. 2003. 'A Mesolithic Settlement at Howick, Northumberland' in *Antiquity* 77: http://antiquity.ac.uk/ProjGall/Waddington/waddington.html

Wickham-Jones, C.R. 2004. 'Structural Evidence' in A. Saville (ed.) *Mesolithic Scotland and its Neighbours: the early Holocene prehistory of Scotland its British and Irish context, and some Northern European perspectives*, 229-242. (Edinburgh: Society of Antiquaries of Scotland)

Woodman, P.C. 1985. *Excavations at Mt. Sandel 1973-1977*. (Belfast: HMSO)

Zvelebil, M. 2003 'People behind the lithics. Social life and social conditions of Mesolithic communities in Temperate Europe' in L. Bevan and J. Moore (eds) *Peopling the mesolithic in a northern environment*, 1-26. (BAR International Series 1157)

AN INTERJECTION

This all seems to keep coming back to points about analogies. Surely we have to be careful about how we use these comparisons. Sometimes you discuss South America, sometimes Australia, and in this chapter there are lots of comparisons with Siberia. Surely the fact that you can't just find one comparison, and work through it systematically, just shows that there's little coherent basis to your argument?

I'd disagree with the last point, but you're right that analogies are vital. Archaeologists have often tried to find ways of making analogy more rigorous: thus people have argued that because environments are similar the analogies are more likely to be valid (as if the fact that it rains in the same months of the year means you are going to think the same things). Alternatively, arguments have been constructed for the validity of analogies where historical continuity might be established. Analogies are also sometimes based on the nature of communities, i.e. that all hunter-gatherers behave in similar ways. Many of these arguments come together in the discussions of northern hunter-gatherer landscapes that have been so common recently: proponents of these models suggest that broad similarities in landscape, economy and, in places, some degree of historical continuity, mean that the analogies are very appropriate. Certainly some of the degree of fit between the ethnographic observations and the archaeological material in Scandinavia is striking. That said, and as noted above, there is a real danger of imposing this model across too broad an area.

All well and good, but can't we just get rid of analogies? Wouldn't we be better off without bringing a load of anthropology into our discussions?

But we can't! Take for example the new timber buildings, where I suggested that there was some disagreement about whether these were ritual structures or houses. This is a distinction between two analogies: the first making comparisons to ethnographic material in arguing that it might be a ritual structure, and the second making a comparison that appeared to be common sense in suggesting it was a house. Structurally, both analogies work in the same way: comparing our unknown (the role of the structure in the past) to something known.

But surely with more evidence we can get by without the analogies altogether?

More evidence will help us choose which analogy is more appropriate, but we can't avoid the role they play in interpretation. We are always moving from the known to the unknown through the establishment of comparisons: the strength of our interpretations is based on how well-founded these comparisons are. If we don't make comparisons, there seems little point to what we do – describing artefact after artefact for its' own sake isn't a particularly valuable thing to be doing.

COMMUNITIES

The focus on this book has been on considering mesolithic lives in Scotland. Yet, all too often in archaeology, discussions are of houses, or animals, or trees, or, worst of all, stone tools. Of course, people float in the background of these discussions, but one of the challenges of archaeological writing is establishing an appropriate balance between the necessary critical attention to the material, and sustaining the visibility of human lives in the past. At times, it often appears we are more interested in the archaeology (56) than the people of the past. Thus far, in this book, I have been using broad themes to integrate discussion of people's lives with the material: in this, the final substantial chapter, that theme is community. Community, however, is a somewhat slippery topic for archaeologists to engage with. Communities are maintained in many different ways, and through differing media. They are transient, existing only in the relationships established between people, and open to competing interpretations.

And yet, concepts of communities of differing kinds have always been present in archaeological discussions of the mesolithic; just in a form that has masqueraded as common sense, and has therefore been unquestioned. For example, writing in the late 1950s, Atkinson felt confident that mesolithic lives in Scotland were of little significance. As discussed in the introduction, dominant models of middle of the twentieth century marginalised hunter-gatherers, describing them as 'strand-loopers', clinging miserably to the edges of the dense woodlands of Scotland. Even so, Atkinson's description is striking:

> The number of individual sites of the mesolithic period now known in Scotland number at least one hundred; but it should not be assumed that these represent more than an exceedingly small population. Many of these sites are marked only by a scatter of flints, which may be no more than the product of a few hours activity by a single flint-knapper, or at best the debris of a temporary camping-site, occupied for a few days by a small band of roving hunters, and then abandoned. Such is the speed at which a skilled flint-knapper works, and such the quantity of waste flint produced in a very short time, that the wanderings of a single family could account, in the space of no more than a few years, for all the finds of microlithic flints in the whole of southern Scotland. ... The mesolithic population of

56 Excavations at the Sands of Forvie, Aberdeenshire. © *G. Warren*

Scotland was exceedingly sparse … until the neolithic colonization the population at any
one time can hardly have exceeded two people for each of the modern counties.
Atkinson, R.J.C. 1962 'Fishermen & Farmers' in S. Piggott (ed.) *The Prehistoric Peoples of
Scotland*, 1-38. (London: Routledge & Kegan Paul, p.6-7)

Of course, few people today would accept such a model of the nature of mesolithic
settlement in Scotland. But Atkinson's vivid depiction of a minimal mesolithic is
redolent with communities: from the single flint-knapper to the band of roving hunters,
a family, and through to population levels. Whilst one might disagree with the particular
interpretations, this account undeniably creates a rich social image of mesolithic
Scotland. The power of such a description derives from the key role of communities in
it. Rather than simply dismissing such accounts, I believe that this forces us to consider
alternative ways of describing mesolithic communities. In considering community, it is
often useful to think in terms of scales: the scales at which people lived their lives, the
distances over which they moved, the extent of the networks which bound them into
wider social obligations. I begin, however, by considering population levels.

POPULATION

Recent years have seen many attempts to derive generalised models of hunter-gatherer
population density, based on environmental or climatic comparisons. These models
typically identify a formula for the density of hunter-gatherers per square kilometre,

and then apply this formula to a given land area. Estimates for Scotland range from 0.09 persons per km² for a high population density giving at total of 7,020 people, to 0.05 persons per km² and 3,900 people for a moderate density, and 0.02 persons per km² and 1560 people for a sparse population.

The estimates obtained are very provisional. Hunter-gatherer population densities vary widely, even within similar ecological contexts, and it is hard to reduce this variation to a formula. As discussed above, Penny Spikins has argued persuasively that many of these so-called facts about hunter-gatherer behaviour drawn from ethnography are actually persistent factoids – or ethno-fictions. Some general models may therefore have little validity. Scotland itself is an exceptionally varied country, from fertile plains and deep sea lochs to high plateaux. It is hard to see how an overall area in km² can reflect this diversity. Scotland's population was clearly not distributed evenly and key areas of ecological diversity are likely to have seen higher settlement levels than, say, the Cairngorm plateaux. The Scottish landscape also changed greatly during the mesolithic, and mesolithic communities changed. Work in behavioural ecology demonstrates that human population levels over time vary greatly, with periods of growth, stability and fall back. Identifying a static 'population' figure in this context is meaningless and seems to pander more to a modern desire for quantification of the past rather than provide any real understanding of that past. The figures provide something misleadingly secure to cling to, in the face of so many unknowns. At best, I would argue that these figures provide a very general range. During the mesolithic the population of Scotland was probably measured in thousands at the most. Any more detailed estimate seems likely to be very misleading. In any case, it is not clear how such abstract figures of 'population' relate to the size of communities in the mesolithic.

Biologists sometimes argue that a population of somewhere between 200-500 is required to form a stable long-term reproductive unit, and this has been associated with a somewhat outdated anthropological concept of a 'tribe', a loose association of people who come together at differing times for trade, exchange, marriage and so on. 'Tribes' (and the word carries unfortunate connotations and is probably best avoided) are sometimes associated with particular areas of land. Anthropologists have also argued that many hunter-gatherers are associated with a kind of social system known as the 'band'. This is a fairly fluid unit of people connected by ties of kinship, who spend much of the year together. The 'band' is often linked to a 'magic number' of about 25 people. This is not a viable population for reproduction, and hence many bands are linked in tribes. Again, these quantifications have been popular in archaeological books – and appear to provide a useful way of thinking about hunter-gatherer communities. One might, for example, use these numbers to consider the population figures above – that a tribe may have focused on the west coast of Scotland, another in the Southern Uplands and so on.

However, there are also many problems here: hunter-gatherers vary greatly in their social organisation. Some live in permanent villages, with hundreds of people, others maintain an exceptionally mobile lifestyle. There is great debate about the extent to which high levels of mobility and a fluid band organisations have been affected by environmental constraints or changes caused by relationships with colonial powers. The value of this specific model of population and community structure to the mesolithic populations of Scotland is not clear.

Traditional approaches to the problem of population in Scotland have therefore focused on generalisations and quantifications. These approaches are problematic, but offer large-scale patterns, against which the data may be seen. One of the difficulties is that the data is rather fragmentary, and the models are, at times, formidably detailed in their construction. In these cases, the models often stand in for the archaeological reality, rather than providing a useful tool to assist in understanding this. In any case, population may be somewhat of a red herring in attempting to understand mesolithic lives in Scotland: especially given the difficulty of pinning down a halfway-decent estimate. People in the mesolithic didn't think in terms of populations across the whole of Scotland – they understood themselves in terms of communities that they were involved in, or had relationships with. Replacing the focus on population with an emphasis on community moves discussion from mathematic models to an understanding of people's lives in the past.

SCALES OF COMMUNITY

At the largest scale the reliance on a microlithic technology in mesolithic Scotland can be seen as part of a European tradition stretching into Russia. Some aspects of the material hint that hunter-gatherers in Scotland belonged to much wider communities. If genuine, for example, the Ahrensburgian, or tanged points, discussed as possible evidence for late-glacial settlement, have much in common with communities across the North Sea basin as a whole. The scanty evidence for early mesolithic stone-tool industries is also very similar across the North Sea basin; with closely comparable formal types found in Germany, northern England and Scotland. Most models of these communities stress great levels of mobility in a general context of new lands opening after deglaciation. Again, there are difficulties with comparisons based solely on tool types, but the hints are that the some of earliest settlers in Scotland were tied into these North Sea communities. It has been argued that the large-scale similarities in material culture at this time indicate very open marriage networks, with community relationships being extended over very long distances.

There are, of course, important differences in particular traditions of tool making that develop over time. England, Wales and Scotland, for example, do not appear to have participated in a shift in microlithic typology to trapezes and rhomboid forms that took place on the continent in the seventh millennium BC. Arguably the creation of the English Channel led to a different trajectory in the British Isles. General models in Britain have suggested that during the course of the mesolithic regional identity became more pronounced, possibly in conjunction with population rise, or sea level rise, or changes in woodland structure. These arguments are very hard to assess in Scotland, where understanding of the details of routines of stone working is too patchy to identify strong regional differences, whereas in England distinctive groups of microliths are considered characteristic of certain regions, or particular patterns of raw material exploitation are reasonably well known.

At times community contacts in the mesolithic of Scotland defy common sense expectations. The issue of links with Ireland, for example, has long been a subject of interest. Ireland lies very close to south-west Scotland – the shortest crossing is 13 miles and the two countries are intervisible (*colour plate 19*) – and whilst the short sea-crossing can be dangerous, there is ample evidence throughout prehistory and history that the seaways provided a vital communication route along the coasts, as well as opportunities for contact with Ireland. Furthermore, and as argued in chapter 4, the mesolithic occupants of Scotland were proficient sailors. Extensive evidence for mesolithic use of islands on the Irish side of the Irish Sea at Dalkey, Sutton, Lambay and Rathlin also indicates routine seafaring. In fact, the presence of large quantities of high-quality large flint on the Antrim coast, and the general scarcity of sources of comparable flint in Scotland has led many archaeologists to expect that communities in Scotland and Ireland were linked in some way. At different times in the twentieth century scholars on both sides of the Irish channel have argued for colonisation from the other island.

And yet the evidence for links between these communities is hard to establish for much of the mesolithic. In the earliest part of the mesolithic in Ireland (around 8000 BC) very similar stone tools to the rest of Europe are discovered – microliths and structured blade working. Although the details are poorly understood, hunter-gatherers in Ireland abandoned microlithic technology at some stage in the seventh millennium BC, opting to use larger flakes and blades, some with simple retouch, instead. This range of tools, which included some distinctive pieces known as 'Bann Flakes', changed over time, but represents a break with wider traditions of manufacture. The same change also happened on the Isle of Man. The reasons for the change in stone-tool manufacture are not clear, but some commentators have suggested that the absence of red deer on Ireland and the Isle of Man may have been significant. This is a possibility, but caches and other structured deposits of stone tools also suggest that the processes of stone-tool production were symbolically significant to the mesolithic populations of Ireland: this implies that the change in technology was not just about practical issues. I argued above that stone working should be considered a form of knowledge, a way of knowing the world; this in turn implies that the differences may have been in more than the ways people held a core, but had wider implications for how people understood the world around them. This is especially striking given the high degree of intervisibility between Ireland and Scotland: what did people think about people on the other side of the water? Furthermore, whilst Ireland's chipped stone tools may have differed from Scotland's, and evidence of direct contact be limited, many other aspects of the archaeology of the periods is similar: with a stress on mobility, repeated occupations of places, the deposition of human bones in midden deposits, even the use of specific types of material culture, such as the bevel-ended tool. Some of the routines of mesolithic life may have remained consistent.

Of course, Scotland is a modern concept, with little significance in understanding the lives of mesolithic hunter-gatherers. Much seems to have linked, for example, the communities of southern Scotland with northern England. I noted in chapter 3 that the Borders has the strongest evidence for the manipulation of forest cover in Scotland, patterns of activity that have strong links to the north of England. Over 30 years ago Helen Mulholland commented that the stone-tool industries of the Tweed Valley were comparable to the north of England. Any given region, of course, changed and shifted over time, not least given environmental changes. Is it therefore possible to gain any sense of the scale of regions?

Issues of scale and links to other areas are often addressed through considering long distance movement or exchange of materials. Much of the material that was exchanged was almost certainly organic, and does not survive; we are therefore limited to discussion of stone. Across Britain and Ireland the existence of small amounts of non-local material has long been recognised. On the south coast of England, for example, artefacts of Portland chert are found up to 250km from their source. Slate and other pebbles from Cornwall are found frequently in Hampshire, over 500km away, and further afield, including some examples that have been moved over 750km. In Ireland, the presence of non-local raw materials is attested at numerous sites, whilst in Europe, hunting and gathering communities established elaborate exchange networks with farmers, with many items moving over great distances.

This evidence has often been interpreted in terms of trade between distinct groups, or simply as an index for the distances people moved in order to obtain raw materials. Danny Hind has argued that understandings of the movement of raw materials in the mesolithic are too simplistic, and that more attention must be paid to the complex social networks in which such objects were exchanged. An argument is frequently made that hunter-gatherers maintain long distance links with other communities in order to provide security in times of hardship: thus in northern Australia, Robert Paton has demonstrated that exchange of *lelira* blades between aboriginal communities appeared to serve no practical function related to the tools themselves, which were often deliberately broken. Paton suggests that the process of exchange provided a means of keeping in touch with distant kin and affines, and, importantly, that sharing knowledge of sources, and the spirits of these places, was a key part of these transactions. As ever with analogies, the point is not that this provides a direct way of making sense of the past, but that it helps provide possibilities. As argued above, stone was much more than simply a useful raw material in the mesolithic: stone was understood within powerful frameworks of meaning, and the presence of exotic raw material, sometimes very visually distinctive, may have been important for a wide variety of reasons. At the very least the presence of small quantities of exotic raw material allows archaeologists to begin to consider the existence of links between different communities in the past, either through exchange, or through journeys to specific sources and the encounters with other people that took place during these trips. By considering these issues, it may be possible to gain some sense of the scales at which people may have lived their lives.

Unfortunately, the evidence from Scotland is stubbornly uninformative in this regard. Much attention has been focused on the movement of materials from particular point-specific sources: for example, a visually distinctive cryptocrystalline silica from Rùm, known as bloodstone, only outcrops on Bloodstone Hill on Rùm (*colour plates 20*

57 Reconstruction of a mesolithic stone working area based on material recovered from the Sands of Forvie, Aberdeenshire. © *A. Braby*

and *21*); its presence in archaeological assemblages away from the island must therefore indicate deliberate movement of the material from Rùm. In the mesolithic, the distances involved here are generally small, bloodstone is found up to approximately 50km from Rùm. These are often interpreted as giving some sense of the distances across which a community routinely moved, rather than indicating long distance trade. The distribution of pitchstone, a distinctive black/green volcanic rock (*colour plate 22*) sourced to a small number of locations on Arran, is probably similar: pitchstone is found much more widely across Northern Britain and Ireland, but the long distance movement is very likely to be neolithic in date and there is no concrete evidence for long distance links in the mesolithic when pitchstone seems, broadly, restricted to the Firth of Clyde. Some claims have been advanced for the presence of imported Yorkshire flint into southern Scotland, especially the Tweed Valley. Unfortunately, these are difficult to sustain.

Rather than indicating exchange and long distance movement, the distribution of certain raw materials for stone tools – Rhum bloodstone and Arran pitchstone – probably offers a good indication of the scales at which mesolithic communities routinely led their lives. These general pictures may also be seen in the east, where it is possible to consider how distinctions between areas may have been tied into people's experiences and identity.

This comes from comparing the contexts for human experience in the north-east (broadly speaking, Aberdeenshire and region) and the south-east (the Tweed). The areas have slightly different distributions of archaeological material. In the Tweed there is clear evidence for a range of mesolithic activity away from immediately riverine contexts, especially in the broken terrain of the middle valley: in environmental terms on an ecotone between the lowland oak forests and upland forests. In the north-east on the Dee and in Strathnairn, despite field survey, no mesolithic activity can be identified away from the riversides. This implies different routines of behaviour and movement in the landscape. Differences in woodland structure in the two areas may have had important implications for the distribution of resources.

Possible distinctions in riverine resources may also have been important. In both areas, the location of sites implies that salmon fishing was an important activity at some times of the year. However, salmon may have run slightly earlier in the north than the south. Although difficult to interpret in absolute terms these differences may have had important influences on the seasonal scheduling of activity, and consequently on the temporal structures within which people in the two areas came to know the world.

Distinctions are also present in the raw material exploited in the areas. The raw material variation in the Tweed Valley, where chert, chalcedony, flint and many other materials were routinely used, was tied up in particular structures of procurement, and ways of learning to work stone (see chapter 5). In the north-east where stone working was dominated by flint, a different distribution of raw materials led to different structures to stone working. Such learnt structures of behaviour, although often tacit, provided an important part of the ways in which people grew up, and learnt their place in the world (57).

Further rhythms may also have been significant; for example, the aurora borealis (northern lights) may have been more frequently visible in the north-east than the south-east, as they are today. Today, as well as being more frequent in winter, the aurora operate on a series of discernible rhythms; for example an 8-16 year solar cycle and a c.27-day cycle. In the north-east today the aurora appear two or more times a month, sometimes displaying for two to three days in a row. It is in many senses a routine part of the night sky, although its character on any given night varies and the most spectacular displays are rare. The absence of light pollution in the mesolithic will have contributed to greater visibility of the aurora and it seems likely that its comparative frequency was an important part of the historical experience of the two areas; in the north-east the aurora was possibly a very much more mundane experience than in the south-east. It is possible that this distinction was also embedded in slight differences in cosmological beliefs between the two areas; many ethnographic studies suggest that appreciable local variation is possible within similar sets of belief and cultures.

These themes are far from exhaustive. I have not, for example, considered the influence of the coast on patterns of activity, but distinctions in landscape use, in some temporal structures and raw materials, point to differences in the character of the historical environment, or landscape, within which people acted in the mesolithic. Although the details refuse resolution there are also indications of differential patterns of learnt behaviour and expectation in those areas. This implies differences in regional identities.

58 Sunset behind the Eildon's, Scottish Borders. © G. Warren

All this discussion about large-scale groups and regions is, of course, at some distance, from understanding people integrated into communities. Anthropologists have also been interested in reconstructing kinship systems for hunter-gatherer groups, understanding how biological relationships between people are modelled, and how this, in turn, provides constraints and potentials for action; especially marriage, but also property rights (of which marriage is sometimes considered a sub-set). Kinship terminology has been studied in great detail, and argued to reveal universal characteristics of classification, or evidence for deep-seated binary structures of thought. These arguments are interesting, and appear to provide a further model for linking populations and communities: that communities should be constructed through family relations. This is certainly a key theme in the organisation of community in many small-scale societies, but it should not be stressed at the expense of other relationships. Furthermore, it is not unusual in such societies that kin terminology is extended to people who manifestly are not biological kin: often the anthropologists themselves are identified within such frameworks. Kin classifications provide a way of structuring the world, but should not be confused with all relationships. Some anthropologists have argued that analysts should focus their attention on 'effective kin' rather than classificatory kin, in other words those people that form the network of community surrounding an individual, some of whom may not be biologically related, or related by marriage, but may play a key role in someone's life. Again, the focus shifts to tasks, and to the immersion of individuals within wider networks: sometimes of family, sometimes of kin, sometimes of affines.

Most of the structural evidence from the Scottish mesolithic, as discussed in the last chapter, remains fairly small-scale, hinting at smaller family or task groups as the key communities in which people spent much of their time. The fire was a vital social context, and large parts of people's lives were assumedly spent in small groups, with all of the intimacies and difficulties this implies. Yet, it is clear that larger scale similarities exist in material culture, and that, at times, contact with larger groups was required. Given this context of fragmenting communities, the difficulty is identifying ways in which larger communities were sustained.

Again, drawing broadly on ethnographic parallels, large-scale gatherings of groups of hunter-gatherers are quite common. These events provided times, and places, where exchanges and marriages could take place, where conflicts could be resolved or the appropriate spiritual support obtained: commonly, these were key times for large-scale ritual activity and gaming. These large gatherings often placed considerable strain on resources in hunting and gathering communities, and they were sometimes scheduled to tie in with seasonal abundances of food or plentiful resources. The large lithic scatters on the rivers of eastern Scotland, especially the Tweed, are interesting in this context. At sites such as Dryburgh Mains, or Rink Farm, many thousands of artefacts have been collected from the surface. The sites are spatially quite extensive and sit in intimate association with key salmon fishing spots. They are probably best interpreted either as long-term repeated points of return, or as extensive short-lived settlements. The assemblages with many microlithic forms, often including those typical of both the early and late mesolithic, alongside a very wide range of raw materials from the surrounding areas, suggest that the sites were in use over the long term. Perhaps, then, these places were, amongst other things, seasonal meeting points for a wider community. The probable presence of the salmon meant that a large gathering could be fed, and rituals and exchanges carried out. Small quantities of chalcedony, carried down from the Cheviots, were exchanged for small amounts of fresh chert, and the chalcedony, with its associated tales, carried up the Tweed with the returning groups. The presence of small amounts of chalcedony at sites in the Peebles area may have originated through just this kind of exchange. At Dryburgh, smaller groups sat on the high bluffs, looking over to the Eildons (58), and discussed how the world had been formed, and how it would continue.

DIFFERENT PEOPLE

Unfortunately, most human societies are far from egalitarian. Inequalities, differences in power, influence and access to goods are common, and sometimes constructed along gender or age categories. Hunting and gathering societies are no different than others in this regard: some hunter-gatherers do live in remarkably fluid, egalitarian communities, where power appears to be related to achievement, and expertise, and differentials in wealth are minimal. But other hunter-gatherers have maintained hereditary leaders and slaves, and accumulated huge personal stores of wealth, which can then be distributed in order to maintain power. The evidence from the mesolithic in Scotland in this regard is slim. There is certainly little to suggest large-scale accumulations of wealth, and as noted above, there is also little evidence of long distance trade, another common feature in attempts to develop and sustain inequalities.

But people were certainly not all alike. Differences in skill and expertise would have been notable, and the subject of much discussion and, most likely, embedded into decision-making processes. Some aspects of this side of community were discussed when examining the skills involved in movement across water. In this regard, it is important to consider the ways in which the body was dressed, or displayed, as a way of marking out differences between people.

The evidence in this regard is limited. No remains of clothes survive, and arguments must be constructed from fragments. Many people's assumptions, and the clothes in many reconstruction drawings, are fairly basic, seemingly comprised of hides and furs – the dominant colour is generally brown. Yet there is a range of evidence that suggests more colour in how people present themselves. For example, salmon skin makes very fine, durable leather that is bright silver in colour. This is not a colour commonly associated with the mesolithic in Scotland. Ochre, a red pigment, is found on numerous mesolithic sites in Scotland. At Morton, 'fingers' of red ochre were discovered, and small grinding bowls found at Fife Ness and Staosnaig may have played a role in preparing pigments. Recent excavations by Caroline Wickham-Jones and Karen Hardy at Sand, on the Inner Sound of Skye, have also shown that mesolithic populations were exploiting dog whelk. Dog whelk is an interesting shellfish, often considered inedible, although there is evidence that it can be eaten. Dog whelk also produces small quantities of a purple dye, and the excavators have raised the cautious possibility that their presence on the midden at Sand indicates preparation of dyes or pigments. Alternative explanations of dog whelk exploitation are possible, but all of this hints at greater uses of colour in mesolithic clothing than often represented – and, of course, creates the potential for divisions between people. Furthermore, many pigments could have been used for tattoos, and it has been suggested that some very small microliths would make ideal tools for applying tattoos. The reconstruction drawings, 45 and 57, offer an alternative vision of mesolithic clothing.

Recent debates have also surrounded the issue of the manufacture of fine hide clothing in the mesolithic in Scotland. As noted above, the use of bevel-ended tools remains subject to debate. Bill Finlayson has proposed that they may have been associated with preparing high quality clothing – the bevel resulting from repeated smoothing of the hide. The presence of these artefacts might, therefore, indicate production and exchange of items that might maintain hierarchy. Different programmes of experimental work are ongoing, and offer partly contradictory results, but the interest in this hypothesis is that it shifts the bevel-ended tools away from being about the subsistence economy, and forces consideration of the production of items that may have marked distinctions between people.

Other examples of decorative material include perforated shells – most notably cowrie shells. Single or double perforated cowries have been found quite widely on Scottish shell middens: at Ulva, Oronsay, Sand and Carding Mill Bay. They are beautiful little artefacts: their collection, perforation and stringing representing an important commitment of time. Cowrie beads are known throughout Europe, as are a range of other beads and pendants: from stone and amber through to a remarkable range

59 Eroding shell midden at Forvie. © *G. Warren*

of perforated animal teeth and human teeth used in Scandinavia, and clearly part of complex symbolic understandings as well as marking out distinctions between people. Little in detail is known about the use of cowries, which in a broader British context are sometimes found in caches inland. There are possible funerary associations for cowrie shells, but beads, and other forms of decoration, may have provided more general ways of marking differences between people. Beads are likely to have been considered significant by virtue of their materials, and the properties these materials were considered to hold.

Such distinctions may have been tied into age grades, or initiations (some elaborate outfits may have been constructed especially for rites of passage such as death), and many are likely to have been structured around gender. Gender has received little explicit attention in mesolithic archaeology until relatively recently, but has always been part of archaeological interpretations, especially reconstruction drawings: thus it is commonly men who are depicted as hunting, with women linked to gathering and maybe shellfish gathering. It is men who are commonly assumed to work stone, and make journeys to sources. And it is women who are associated with structures and to 'domestic' tasks. Put simply, these are assumptions with little basis in the character of the archaeological record. Clive Bonsall, for example, has argued on the basis of ethnographic evidence that the shell middens of western Scotland were used by women and children as special purpose processing camps for marine resources, whilst men undertook other tasks elsewhere. The absence of microliths from the middens in this argument is seen as linking particular forms of technology to particular tasks and to particular groups of people: in particular here again an association between retouched tools and male tasks is implied, despite many criticisms of such models in the wider literature. Arguments associating genders with tasks are often hard to assess in detail. In this example, it is possible that such a gendered division of labour did exist in the past, but Bonsall makes little attempt to identify evidence from the middens that would allow him to really argue for the presence of women and children. For example, it might be possible to analyse the lithic assemblages and identify apprenticeship, thus providing a stronger argument for the presence of children. In the absence of this evidence the claim is simply the application of an ethnographically derived model. This model assumes that gender roles in the past were similar to those seen in the present, and provides a template for understanding them. Most importantly, as with so many models of mesolithic society, the generalisation stands in for the detail, and overwrites it: where, for example, are the funerary associations of middens in this discussion?

In an excellent review paper, Nyree Finlay has provided a robust critique of notions of gender in mesolithic archeology in Britain and Ireland. Finlay argues strongly that gender is one of a number of axes of difference in mesolithic communities: age, sex, skill and so on. Gender is not essentially reduced to biological sex, and must be understood through the performance and negotiation of particular tasks and roles as part of wider sets of relationships, or taskscapes. As outlined above, Finlay's development of multiple authorship as a way of considering microlithic technology provides one way of understanding the integration of different people in particular projects and objects. Gender therefore provides one of the frames around which community is woven, and the construction and reconstruction of these relationships must be understood as a bringing together of different materials and possibilities.

For example, and returning to middens, it is clear that these sites should not simply be about women and children. Middens (59) represent the outcome of an enormous suite of activity. Fishing, for example, appears to have involved the use of traps. These traps themselves required manufacture, this in turn necessitating their own taskscape of particular activities, gathering of reeds or harvesting of hazel, for example. As discussed above, evidence from Forvie strongly implies that these tasks were embedded in other tasks, such as up-tooling of flint. To consider all of these tasks and their associations female is too reductive. As well as fishing, hunting is evidenced on the middens as well as, possibly, the manufacture of clothes, the treatment of the dead, lighting of fires, flint working and of course, the collection of shellfish. Middens can therefore be understood as a place integrating the varied tasks characteristic of mesolithic life. Some of these tasks may have been gendered, or age specific, but it was only in their integration that the place made sense as a whole, that the midden worked. Middens created an assemblage of associations in one place, and as people moved from and to the midden they would bring and carry associations with them.

Of course, these associations are true of all mesolithic sites, not simply middens. Middens have the preservation that demonstrates assemblages of different tasks created in the past, but similar integrations would have characterised all mesolithic sites in Scotland. In such a situation, to identify some tasks as female, and others as male, seems inappropriate. Gender provided one of the main axes around which distinctions within a society could be structured, but it is also important recognise that the ways in which these misunderstandings might be manifested in any particular context vary greatly. The archaeologist's task in understanding gender is not to separate male and female, or young and old, but to understand how such differentiations made senses of community possible.

OTHER COMMUNITIES

This discussion of community has been rather unbalanced thus far, for I have only considered the community of living humans. As discussed above, many hunter-gatherers make little categorical distinction between humans, animals and other aspects of the natural world. These things all play their part in a 'relational epistemology'. Can we find any evidence of these community ties?

The best evidence comes from the Oronsay middens. As noted above, some of these middens include small quantities of human bone: finger and toe bones, and some skull fragments. Often, this has been interpreted in terms of excarnation, or leaving the body to deflesh over time, a practice with strong neolithic parallels in Britain. However, Chantal Conneller has argued that parallels can be drawn between the representation of human and animal bones on the middens: in that the same parts of the body are frequently present. This seems to suggest that the processes by which human bone were incorporated into the middens was rather more complex than just excarnation. Conneller argues that 'these lines of evidence suggest that parallels were being drawn between the human body and analogous animal body parts'. Most strikingly, at Cnoc Coig a human hand was placed onto a seal flipper. This remarkable deposit implies considerable continuity between the animal and human worlds, through the anatomically precise parallel drawn between a hand and flipper. Seal (*colour plate 23*) was the dominant mammal in the faunal assemblage at Cnoc Coig, and the association between human and animal here did not appear to stop people hunting seals, including very young pups. It is also interesting in this context that the isotopic analysis of human bone from Cnoc Coig indicates a diet wholly dominated by marine foods: of all the places where an equivalency might be made between a human and a seal, this site seems very appropriate.

At Cnoc Coig in particular, and the Oronsay middens in general, an equivalency of some kind appears to be established between human and animal, suggesting, in part, that these were both considered as part of the same community. Further evidence is hard to come by: the treatment of whales outlined in the last chapter may indicate some similar concerns. Looking further afield offers hints of the character of these relationships, but it is hard to accept these parallels as models for Scotland. Three thousand years earlier in north Yorkshire carefully prepared frontlets of red deer antlers had been perforated so that they could be worn on a human head. Often interpreted as either a hunting disguise, or a ceremonial headdress, Conneller has recently argued that this act draws an equivalency between human and animals, and may be part of ritual where the human takes on the form of a deer.

Relational epistemologies also, however, stretch beyond humans and animals to encompass trees, stones, shells and a wide range of other materials. As noted in chapter 3, for many forest dwelling hunter-gatherers the forest is considered as a parent. A key area of future work on the mesolithic should be a fine-grained focus on materiality, trying to pick apart how different materials may have been embedded in, and helped to construct, particular systems of meaning. As well as animals, of course, the community extended temporally, to include the dead and the ancestors. At times, mesolithic activity was redolent with associations of the dead. As noted above, paths, carvings and clearings may have outlived individuals, and been inherited as people grew up. Some middens were one of the most dramatic examples of congealed human activity – generation after generation of the same kind of activity. Be it feasting or famine, the key theme here is that middens grew through repeated behaviour – that a visit to this place reminded you of those generations gone before, who had also visited here, and done more or less the same thing.

In Britain in general, funerary practices appear to have changed considerably during the mesolithic and to have had an important aspect of regional variation. Cremations are known from Ireland, with grave goods, whilst burials of whole and partial bodies are found in caves in south-west England and Wales. Chantal Conneller, in a stimulating review of this often ignored material, has argued that disarticulation is a key theme, and that the combinations of human bones with animal bones and particular places through the creation of new assemblages of material was not so much about death, as about communities of the living creating new possibilities and ways of thinking. The small amount of funerary evidence from Scotland is broadly in keeping with this, and also implies that the manipulation of the bones of the dead was practiced, and this in turn suggests that links and relationships with the dead were maintained by the living through the use of the material remains of those dead.

REVIEW

Community is often perceived to be a nebulous aspect of prehistory, and yet, this discussion has made some progress in considering mesolithic communities. Thinking about the largest scales of people's lives has not been helpful in this regard. For example, it is clear that at a very large scale, the mesolithic occupants of Scotland were part of an extensive series of communities across most of north-western Europe who manufactured and used microlithic stone tools. Such statements are, however, rather problematic: on the one hand, they are truisms, but, more importantly, they do not help assess how meaningful these scales were to people's lives. Population levels, with all their problems, are too abstract to really inform about people's daily sense of self and community.

Our examples have suggested that community was not stable, and changed according to contexts, places and tasks. Communities changed significantly over the long term. Communities were divided internally, but can only be perceived of in terms of the reintegration of these different elements. Communities were not limited to humans, but networks of relatedness extended to incorporate animals and the dead, and most likely, many, many other aspects of the world.

FURTHER READING

Many of the themes in this chapter have been touched on already in discussions. Models of population and breeding networks are outlined in Smith (1992) and the population figures are taken from a recent working party statement (Gardiner 1999). A recent discussion of the change in Irish stone working is found in Costa et al. (2004), whilst Saville (2003) and McCartan (2003) offer recent reviews of the relationships between Ireland, Scotland and the Isle of Man. Hind (1998) and Paton (1994) both offer perspectives on the movement of raw materials. Discussions of gender bias and how to (and not to) write a gendered archaeology of the mesolithic are in Finlay (2000, forthcoming). Bonsall's gendered shell middens are in his discussion of the Obanian (1996). Conneller's papers on burial and the body are essential reading (2004, forthcoming).

Bonsall, C. 1996. 'The "Obanian Problem": coastal adaptation in the Mesolithic of Western Scotland' in T. Pollard and A. Morrison (eds) *The Early Prehistory of Scotland*, 165-182. (Edinburgh: Edinburgh University Press)

Conneller, C.J. 2004. 'Becoming deer: corporeal transformations at Star Carr' in *Archaeological Dialogues* 11(1): 37-56

Conneller, C.J. forthcoming. 'Death' in C. Conneller and G. Warren (eds) *Mesolithic Britain and Ireland: new approaches.* (Stroud: Tempus Publishing)

Costa, L.J., Sternke, F. and Woodman, P.C. 2004 'Microlith to macrolith: the reasons behind the transformation of production in the Irish Mesolithic' in *Antiquity* 79: 19-33

Finlay, N. 2000. 'Deer Prudence' in *Archaeological Review from Cambridge* 17: 67-79

Finlay, N. forthcoming, 'Gender' in C. Conneller and G. Warren (eds) *Mesolithic Britain and Ireland: new approaches.* (Stroud: Tempus Publishing)

Gardiner, J. 1999. *Research Frameworks for the Palaeolithic and Mesolithic of Britain and Ireland.* (Salisbury: Sarum Graphics/Prehistoric Society)

Hind, D. 1998. 'Chert use in the Mesolithic of Northern England' in *Assemblage: University of Sheffield graduate student journal of archaeology* 4. http://www.shef.ac.uk/assem/4/.

McCartan, S. 2003 'Mesolithic Hunter-Gatherers in the Isle of Man: adaptations to an island environment?' in L. Larsson et al. (eds) 2003 *Mesolithic on the move: papers presented at the Sixth International Conference on the Mesolithic in Europe, Stockholm 2000*, 331-339. (Oxford: Oxbow)

Paton, R. 1994. Speaking through stones: a study from Northern Australia. *World Archaeology* 26(2): 172-184

Saville, A. 2003. 'Indications of regionalisation in Mesolithic Scotland' in L. Larsson et al. (eds) 2003 *Mesolithic on the move: papers presented at the Sixth International Conference on the Mesolithic in Europe, Stockholm 2000*, 340- 350. (Oxford: Oxbow)

Smith, C. 1992. *Late Stone Age Hunters of the British Isles.* (London: Routledge)

AN INTERJECTION

At the start of all of this, I really didn't think that we'd be able to say much in detail about people's lives in the mesolithic. You've managed to convince me that there are interesting ways of approaching the material; but this all seems very fragmentary. I think I'd get quite frustrated looking at this kind of subject: wouldn't you rather look at a period with more evidence to be able to build these stories in more detail?

Another good point. Firstly, it is important to note that there is a lot of very good work carried out on other archaeological periods, focusing on very similar themes to those in this book: how people understood the landscape around them, and what this might have meant in terms of their identity, and the ways in which they acted in particular situations. But why the mesolithic? Yes, of course, the material is fragmentary, and as I argued at the outset, it will probably always be: there are issues of chronological resolution to be taken into consideration, as well as the importance of change within hunting and gathering communities. And yes, sometimes a little more detail in our evidence would be helpful.

Exactly: wouldn't you be better studying the neolithic or Bronze Age? Your interpretations could be much richer.

But that's part of the point! There is a general preconception that mesolithic archaeology doesn't have the richness of later periods. And yes, there undoubtedly are differences in the nature of the material available to us: but as I've argued throughout this, our material can tell us useful things, and, in fact, trying to make it do so is a wonderful intellectual challenge. This, in itself, is one of the reasons I love the study of the mesolithic: I came into archaeology with lots of grand ideals about the need to study people, not generalisations; trying to work these through with a limited range of material is never anything short of challenging. I'm also drawn to the study of mobile communities.

There is also the important point that the mesolithic experience of Scotland was significant: covering over 5,000 years. This needs to be part of the story of Scotland. Furthermore, 'hunter-gatherers' play an important part in modern systems of thought: particularly in the kind of crude evolutionary models we often use to consider change over time. Trying to discuss those hunter-gatherers in as human a way as possible hopefully challenges some of these preconceptions.

EPILOGUE: THINKING ABOUT
REAL CONDITIONS

This book has been much longer in the writing than initially anticipated and it has changed character over the time of its growth. I began work on it in 2002, soon after the completion of my Doctorate, and at the time envisaged a book based heavily on my thesis, with some more imaginative and intimate sections highlighting the character of people's lives during the mesolithic. Everything, it appeared, should be quite straightforward. Life, as so often, laid waste to these plans: I was lucky enough to get a job at University College Dublin, and we moved to Dublin in September of 2002. The pressures of a new job, in a new country, made progress on the book hard: I was able to write a chapter over the Christmas holidays in 2002, another in 2003 and another in 2004: but little more.

Alongside the competing demands on my time, I think the delays in writing the book also reflected a growing sense of doubt in my mind about how it was going to work. Put simply, I became concerned about the grounding of some of the more interpretative sections. Recently, the use of empathy as a way of humanising the archaeology of the mesolithic has become more and more common. Sometimes based on weak claims of human universals or the structure of the brain, these accounts are popular, but also problematic. I have spent some time trying to situate my archaeological practice in relation to such accounts. This process of exploration has led to new directions and new ideas: and this book reflects that.

The end of this book perhaps provides a good context to explore these doubts about empathy in a little more detail. The clearest statement of these recent trends comes from Steven Mithen, a prolific and popular archaeological writer as well as the overall director of the Southern Hebrides Mesolithic Project. The project's recent publication includes a short closing chapter: *Finale: the Mesolithic Experience in Scotland*. This paper draws on Mithen's experiences of working in the Southern Hebrides as a way of understanding the mesolithic experience. Similarly, in his *After the Ice* a time-traveller serves as a convenient literary device, allowing Mithen to use empathy to imaginatively describe life in varied mesolithic locations. Mithen offers a justification for his use of empathy in the *Mesolithic Experience* paper. Drawing on some arguments from evolutionary psychology – broadly speaking a discipline studying how the structure of the mind has supposedly been affected by evolution – Mithen argues that our modern brains are essentially hunter-gatherer minds. Furthermore, he suggests, places like western Scotland, where one can be close to nature, are the best places to try and make these connections with the hunter-gatherer mind. Thus 'mesolithic hunter-gatherers and twenty-first century academics can and do share a fundamentally similar experience of the world'. Mithen acknowledges that such arguments leave him open to 'criticism if not ridicule' and stresses that these approaches are included because he feels the mesolithic experience is missing from the rest of the report. Empathy is Mithen's methodology for humanising the mesolithic in Scotland, buttressed by claims about human universals. My aim here is not to ridicule, but to consider whether these approaches are appropriate.

This is not the context in which to open a detailed discussion on evolution and the structure of the brain. However, it is appropriate to note some concerns. I would argue that rather than having aspects of our characters fixed in advance of our development, humans grow in very different ways in different contexts. The ways in which the processes of development from foetus to adult (or 'developmental cooking' to use one popular metaphor) take place within particular environments are vital to understanding the interplay between inheritance and variation. Humans have huge potentials for variation, and learn to live in and deal with many different challenges: different landscapes, different systems of behaviour, different diets. To fix upon one aspect of our identity – to claim we have hunter-gatherer brains for example – seems to me misguided. Furthermore, I think that Mithen's argument that it is possible to have a mesolithic experience in natural contexts is also dangerous. As stated throughout this book, nature and culture are understood in highly variable ways across different groups of people. How 'natural' the landscapes of Scotland might be is open to great debate: centuries of management have greatly affected the distribution of plants and animals. Scotland's contemporary landscapes are represented and contested within a finely constructed discourse of wilderness; and perception of them in this way is not that of a native – but of someone who visits. There is considerable danger that such accounts are affected by powerful cultural influences that make open spaces and the sight of wildlife romantic experiences. Furthermore, it is important to note that the archaeological experience of landscape is a very specific one (60-62, *colour plate 24*).

I firmly believe that human variation is greater than many arguments about empathy allow; that the ways in which people made and make sense of the world are multitudinous, and that this means that people's experiences differ widely. This is not to argue that we cannot understand each other in different contexts. Pálsson argues strongly, for example, that the best way of achieving understanding of different approaches to life is through pragmatics: through daily action, dialogue and involvement. Translation between different groups or traditions, in this sense, is not the attempt to render the alien into a different language, but arises from the art of everyday getting on in the world, making sense of people around us through our mutually constituting involvement in each other, something we all do every day of our lives. This does not imply that there are no differences between people's experience of the world. It only implies that most differences could be overcome by the co-presence of people willing to make the effort to learn by becoming actively

Above: 60 Informal fieldwalking
at the important mesolithic site of
Springwood Park, River Tweed.
© *G. Warren*

Right: 61 View of excavations at the
Dookits, Scottish Borders, 1998.
© *G. Warren*

62 Excavations at Kinloch, Rùm. © *Caroline Wickham-Jones*

involved in each other's worlds. Steve Mithen walking on a hillside is not having 'a mesolithic experience', but if someone were to involve him in one, nothing in his twenty-first century being would necessarily stop him understanding and sharing in many aspects of that experience. This, in turn, suggests that what we should be focusing on should not be human universals, and empathy, but on understanding how people came to know the world around them. Broadly, I am influenced by wider trends in archaeological practice, especially an interest in what have been termed 'the real conditions' of past lives: or, as John Barrett and Kathy Fewster have outlined. 'how the world was actually and knowledgably occupied and the consequences of that occupation'.

This book has tried to be an introduction to the mesolithic of Scotland that refuses to follow the path of empathy. I also decided to avoid the use of short fictional sections to provide romances of those mesolithic lives. Instead, I have been attempting to develop an emphasis on the conditions under which mesolithic people in Scotland came to know the world around them. Even in its more imaginative sections, such as the discussion of seascapes, my intent has been to consider how particular material conditions contributed to ways of understanding the world. Similarly, my discussions of stone working focused on the development of skilled practice and the integration of particular tasks.

The people of mesolithic Scotland came to know the world through play, not least, play when children. They learnt that particular rocks could be used in certain ways, and that certain spirits were involved in that process: that the spirits helped you work rock in some ways, but not others. Children learnt that many tasks needed to be carried out in the appropriate fashions to live in the proper way. They learnt that deciding when these tasks should take place, and which ones were more important, was a cause of much debate. They learnt who their relatives were; and whom they could call upon in times of trouble. Changes in the weather over the years were noted, discussed, and integrated into wider rhythms.

They learnt that some materials could only be deposited in special places in the landscape. Others were less constrained in their actions. They learnt how to make these judgements themselves. They learnt to move through the woods spotting the vast array of materials that were there to help them: from stones and wood to mushrooms and carvings. Children learnt about the spirits that surrounded them and must be offered gifts. Other spirits were communicated with through moving bones. Food needed gathering and preparing for visitors, and fine clothes might be worn to impress them. Particular skills were learnt: of tracking, of sewing. They learnt how to recognise the marks of previous visitors: and to differentiate between those who had visited last year, and the presence of the spirits. How many people were needed to build the required structure? How could they be fed? They recognised how the levels of the sea had changed, and debated the reasons why.

All of these competencies, and many, many more, were drawn upon as the inhabitants of mesolithic Scotland grew in the world, and made decisions about where to go and what to do. And all of these skills were used in different contexts, as they went about their daily lives, actively creating and sustaining rich, specific and varied understandings of the world. It is my hope that this book has offered the modern reader some hints of these understandings and those lives.

FURTHER READING

Mithen's discussions of empathy are found in publications in 2000, 2003 and 2004. Pálssons consideration of translation and cross-cultural understanding is in the dense but stimulating *Textual Life of Savants*. The discussion of the real conditions of past lives draws upon a recent paper by Barrett and Fewster (2000), the quote is from p.29. Lesley McFadyen's response (2000) is also important.

Barrett, J.C. and Fewster, K.J. 2000. 'Intimacy and Structural Transformation: Giddens and Archaeology' in C. Holtorf and H. Karlsson (eds) *Philosophy and Archaeological Practice: perspectives for the 21st century*, 25-33. (Göteberg: Bricoleur Press)

McFadyen, L. 2000. 'Comment: the trouble with the "real" thing' in C. Holtorf and H. Karlsson (eds) *Philosophy and Archaeological Practice: perspectives for the 21st century*, 34-37. (Göteberg: Bricoleur Press)

Mithen, S.J. 2000. 'Finale: the Mesolithic Experience' in S.J. Mithen (eds) *Hunter-gatherer landscape archaeology: The Southern Hebrides Mesolithic Project 1988-1998*, 627-633. (Cambridge: McDonald Institute for Archaeological Research)

Mithen, S.J. 2003. *After The Ice: A Global Human History*. (Weidenfield & Nicholson)

Mithen, S.J. 2000. 'The "Mesolithic Experience" in Scotland' in A. Saville (ed.) *Mesolithic Scotland and its Neighbours: the Early Holocene Prehistory of Scotland, its British and Irish context and some Northern European Perspectives*, 243-260. (Edinburgh: Society of Antiquaries of Scotland)

Pálsson, G. 1995. *The Textual life of Savants: Ethnography, Iceland and the Linguistic Turn*. (Harwood Academic Publishers)

INDEX

Entries in bold refer to illustrations